STROKING FOREHEAD TECHNIQUE

This is an excellent method of inducing hypnosis. As the hands are drawn over the subject's forehead, it is suggested that she will fall into a deep state of hypnosis. This procedure has a pleasant physiological effect on the subject.

THE HOUR GLASS TECHNIQUE

The subject is instructed to watch the sand as it falls from the top to the bottom segment of the glass. She is told that as the upper part of the receptacle empties, she will find her eyes becoming extremely heavy, and that she will fall into a deep somnambulistic state as her eyes close.

CHEVREUL'S PENDULUM TEST

In spite of her desire to keep the chain immobile as instructed, she is in the grip of a subconscious compulsion to revolve it, due to the hypnotic suggestion that she will be unable to prevent herself from doing so.

FLASHLIGHT TECHNIQUE

As the light of the pen light is shined into the subject's eyes, deep hypnosis is suggested to her. This technique is an excellent one since both the light and the strained position of the eyes tend to hasten the onset of fatigue, which paves the way for the consequent hypnotic state.

MIRROR TECHNIQUE FOR SELF-HYPNOSIS

Here the subject is hypnotizing herself with the aid of a hand mirror. As she looks into the mirror she gives herself hypnotic suggestions, which take effect after she finishes the count of three.

FALLING BACK TEST

The subject here is beginning to fall backwards due to suggestion. Notice how the head is raised causing the subject to be slightly off balance, and how the hypnotist has placed one foot back to brace himself for the fall of the subject.

FALLING FORWARD TEST

Here we observe the correct position for the falling forward test. With this test successfully completed, the hypnotist assures the subject of her susceptibility to hypnosis. It is suggested to the subject that she gaze intently into the hypnotist's left eye, as the subject does so she is told she will find herself falling forward.

A SMALL PICTURE OF THE POWERS HYPNODISC

The above picture shows the Powers hypnodisc. Its original size is twelve inches in diameter. It is placed on a phonograph turntable and as the subject looks at it, the hypnotist suggests hypnosis.

ADVANCED TECHNIQUES

of

HYPNOSIS

A Professional Hypnotist
Reveals New Procedures for Inducing
Both Deep and Self-Hypnosis

by
MELVIN POWERS
Author
Dynamic Thinking
Hypnotism Revealed
The Science of Hypnotism
A Practical Guide to Self-Hypnosis
Mental Power Thru Sleep Suggestion
Self-Hypnosis, Its Theory, Technique and Application

Published by
Melvin Powers
WILSHIRE BOOK COMPANY
12015 Sherman Road
No. Hollywood, California 91605
Telephone: (213) 875-1711

Printed by

HAL LEIGHTON PRINTING COMPANY
P.O. Box 3952
North Hollywood, California 91605
Telephone: (213) 983-1105

Printed in the United States of America

Library of Congress Catalog Card Number 53-26107

ISBN 0-87980-002-X

CONTENTS

FOREWORD

THE PRACTICE of hypnosis is as old as history itself. This fascinating art was first introduced to the world in the ancient land of Egypt, and has persisted to the present day. It was, doubtless, passed on through the priests of Egypt, Persia, and the Levites, and later spread to the Greeks and Romans, who kept its fire aglow so that Europe could benefit from its warmth at a later date through the experiments of such friends of man as Mesmer, Charcot, Berhnheim, and others, who did so much to contribute to our deeper understanding of this dynamic force.

Hypnosis is not a mystic rite, nor is it a stage trick performed solely for the edification, and delight of an audience. It has been a part of man's history too long to be looked upon as mere entertainment. It is, primarily, a technical means of helping those who are in distress because of subjective fears, or pressures of whatever kind, be they of a mental, spiritual, or physical nature. It is with this serious purpose, and with the scientific implementation of hypnosis, that we are concerned in this book.

There have been many books written on the therapeutic value of hypnosis. Numerous volumes have dealt with its history, and many more have been concerned with its various phenomena. There has, however, been comparatively little written about the actual technique of inducing the hypnotic state. Since this phase of hypnosis has been so woefully neglected, we have not had the rapid technical development our vital science so rightfully deserves. This volume is designed to remedy that lack.

I have personally known psychologists who had given up using hypnosis solely because of their inability to effect the hypnotic state in their patients; but who, when at last were properly shown how easily this state could be induced in most subjects, were finally unanimous in their enthusiastic acceptance of its therapeutic value.

This book is dedicated to those who aspire to a fuller understanding of hypnotic procedures. It is my purpose to show you, the reader, how to develop any individual into a receptive, hypnotic subject, and to give you the necessary understanding and knowledge required to achieve this end. You will also be instructed in the use of my original techniques, which have proven to be so wonderfully effective in my long experience as a professional hypnotist. A careful reading of the book will not only be rewarding because of the wealth of information contained in it, but will also assure the reader maximum professional efficiency in the exciting, and fascinating practice of professional hypnosis.

Melvin Powers

12015 Sherman Road
No. Hollywood, California 91605

CHAPTER I

What Every Hypnotist Should Know

IN MY OPINION, the hypnotist must firstly be a person of the highest integrity, who is ever aware of his responsibilities to his clients. He must be firmly grounded in the study and understanding of psychology and its techniques; of affable address; of sympathetic attitude; of pleasant and reassuring manner; of calm understanding and patience; so that the total impression of his personality, inevitably creates the favorable rapport that is so essential to the success of the able hypnotist. The hypnotist must above all have complete confidence in himself and his technical efficiency, since to be effective, it is necessary that he speak with the surest authority, so that he can control the subject completely.

Even if you chance to be a beginner in this field, you must still proceed in a manner that will instill complete confidence in your subject, since it is not likely that you will be successful if the subject becomes aware that you are a novice in the field of hypnosis, for no one is inclined to be the first subject of an amateur hypnotist, no matter how enthusiastic he may be. You must never fumble in your procedure, and if questioned, you must have a confident and ready answer for whatever question that may arise in the subject's mind. To say, "I do not know" to a question, is to destroy whatever confidence the subject may have in you, thus eliminating any possibility of achieving the harmony so necessary to successful hypnosis. In the event that the correct answer is not known, it is still necessary to offer a convincing explanation, so that no loss of prestige would affect the successful conclusion of hypnosis.

It is further always important to remember that mistakes will be made, no matter how many books have been read on the subject of hypnosis. It is the purpose of this book to make the hypnotic procedures so clear that errors in methodology will never occur at all, or, at least, very seldom, if the book's principles are conscientiously applied by the reader. It is, above all, the actual practice that creates the skill and proficiency of the successful hypnotist. It is, therefore, advisable that the budding hypnotist find as many subjects as he can, so that he can most quickly arrive at that stage of proficiency which will mark him as an efficient technician. It is my suggestion, if you are a novice, that your first subject be someone who is not too well known to you. In fact, a total stranger would be best, since not being aware of your apprenticeship in hypnosis, he would respond with more alacrity than your friends, or members of your family. You would thus be given a greater opportunity to become familiar with the hypnotic techniques and to develop your skill to the fullest possible degree of virtuosity.

Once your reputation as a hypnotist is assured, the prestige which redounds from this distinction will predispose others to seek you out. In my experience, as a professional hypnotist, I have observed that it was particularly those persons who had been referred to me by my former patients, that made the most excellent subjects for hypnosis, since they have been pre-conditioned, as it were, by the enthusiasm of those beneficiaries, who had come under my influence in the past. These new subjects, therefore, having become favorably disposed toward my person and reputation, very quickly fell under the control of my hypnotic suggestions. Since they had already been "sold" on my competence as a hypnotist, it was only necessary to maintain their lively confidence in my reputation, and to proceed quickly to the conclusion of the hypnotic state with them. With such subjects, it was not necessary to spend either time or energy on the pre-hypnotic talk, since these were not required, due to the favorable condition that had been created in advance through fore-knowledge of my reputation. I, therefore, immediately proceeded to the actual hypnosis; working as rapidly as I could to induce the deep hypnotic state, which is the goal of every hypnotist. This procedure had obviously been made much easier for me, due to the advanced state of suggestibility with which these subjects came to me, as a result of their having been referred to me by those former subjects, with whom I had already consummated successful hypnosis. It, merely, remained for me to take the fullest advantage of this heightened susceptibility to hypnosis

[17]

that had already been created in these persons by my former subjects. This I did, and always with the greatest success.

I would like, at this time, to make, what I feel is, an interesting observation. It is only on very rare occasions that I meet a person who insists that he is an easy subject to hypnotize. On the contrary, I find, almost always, that the prospective subject protests his inability to do so. When asked for a cogent reason, however, he is usually unable to offer one; stating merely that he feels it, and, therefore, it is so, as far as he is concerned. At this point, it is necessary to explain that almost everybody feels the same way at this stage of the procedure, and that he, too, doubtlessly will make a good subject. If the subject still persists, protesting that he has too strong a will for hypnotic manipulation, congratulate him on such a possession, and point out how this will-power can be used to bring about a proper state for the induction of hypnosis. If, on the other hand, your subject protests that he has a weak will, point out to him that hypnosis is dependent neither upon a strong nor a weak will for its effect, and that all that is really required of him is his fullest cooperation in the procedure. It is well, at this point, to ask him whether he is willing to cooperate wholeheartedly. If he agrees to do so, and he usually will, say that success is assured. It becomes clear, then, that the method employed depends rather upon the peculiarities of the individual, rather than on any impersonal or rigid procedure. It is this type of flexibility which makes for the most successful and resourceful practice in the field of hypnosis.

Even the subject, who earnestly desires to be hypnotized, does not always respond favorably, due to excessive tension. He is like the person who wants to sleep, but cannot do so, because his intense desire creates a nervous tension which prevents it. So it is with the subject, who wants to be hypnotized so much that he can't relax in the process, thereby making hypnosis impossible. The hypnotist must, therefore, soothe the subject, relaxing him by telling him that he is a very good subject, and that he will soon certainly go under hypnosis as he concentrates on what is said to him, and as soon as the influences of the hypnotic suggestions affect him. These suggestions will ease him, and make him more tractable. It is absolutely necessary to employ these measures, before beginning the actual induction of hypnosis, to insure success! It will save many hours of futile labor. The subject is informed that he is first being conditioned to hypnosis, and that suggestions will be used to bring him to a greater depth of passivity. Tell him what he is to expect from each stage, since this information plays an important role in the eventual induction. He must be invited to watch for the appropriate signs, and to interpret them as they occur. This will convince him that progress has been made, and that he will soon be under the full effects of the hypnotic state.

Most of us reach the condition of sleep in stages. That is, we do not attain full sleep immediately, but enter into a progression of varying depths of unconsciousness until we fall into the state of deep sleep. Similar conditions prevail in hypnosis. The subject comes to the hypnotic state by degrees, also. While it is true, though with the exceptional few sleep does come immediately, hynotism, like sleep, normally is achieved through the above mentioned stages. It is, therefore, the task of the hypnotist to lead the subject expertly and unerringly through these stages to the final goal of deep hypnosis.

CHAPTER II

The Psychological Approach and Technique

THE AVERAGE subject will go under hypnosis within the period of five minutes, if the hypnotist is fully acquainted with the proper procedure. The matter of timing is of the utmost importance. If an attempt is made to induce hypnosis before the subject is ready for it, failure is inevitable. The subject must first be saturated with the idea of being hypnotized, and his mind must be orientated to its fullest acceptance. I know from experience, that the average person is excessively skittish during his first exposure to hypnosis. He may not only become nervous, but may also be excessively distracted by the technique. This is particularly true of those who, having a prior interest in hypnosis, have done some reading on the subject. These persons, being easily diverted, must be prevailed upon to respond with the greatest concentration to the ministrations of the hypnotist to insure the best effects.

The psychologist must develop a positive transference with his patient for successful treatment. The hypnotherapist requires even greater transference before he can attempt hypnosis. If he should fail in his first attempt, he may leave a negative reaction with his patient which may be extremely difficult to overcome. It is, therefore, better to proceed deliberately, gaining the subject's complete confidence in the process, while at the same time obtaining a greater understanding of his problem, so that the procedure employed will best suit the particular needs of the patient.

It is a good policy, in my opinion, to capitalize on the ideas and information your subjects may have on the subject of hypnosis. A technique I have found useful in my office, is to take a crystal ball from my pocket and show it to the subject. I ask him if he knows for what purpose it is used. Invariably, I am told that it is used to induce the hypnotic state. It is used, I am further informed, as a point of concentration. Having gained my point, I say, "That is correct. I am now going to use it to induce a deep, hypnotic state in you." The subject has thus already related the crystal ball to hypnosis, and in this manner, has already convinced himself not only of its relationship, but also its effectiveness. After all, he had, himself, stated that the crystal ball was used to induce the hypnotic state. He now has the "mental set" to prove it, both to me, and to himself. This procedure is far superior, in my judgment, than merely saying, "I am now going to induce the hypnotic state by using the Powers hypnotic crystal ball." The latter method, of course, can be employed, but I have found that the previous technique is infinitely more effective.

Through the use of the crystal ball, we can cause the muscular fatigue of the eyelids, thus creating a condition of drowsiness that is a very useful means of leading the subject into the hypnotic state. It is essential to keep this fact in mind, whatever technique is employed. This is done through suggestion and the concentration of the subject's eyes on the crystal ball, or other objects chosen by the technician, such as the

"Hypnodisc". Once this has been achieved, the subject's mind is more receptive to the other suggestions that follow. He is not told that the physiological effect of weariness is due to the strained concentration of his eyes on whatever object the hypnotist has selected for him to look at; but rather, that they feel heavy, watery, and tired because of the technician's suggestions to the subject.

What do you suppose is the single greatest mental block to hypnosis? My fifteen years of experience in the field of hypnosis has taught me that it is the fear of revealing something that the subject does not consciously wish to divulge. The matter may be a trivial or important one that the subject has kept suppressed, or it may be something which he feels too ashamed or bashful to relate to anyone. Fearing that the hypnotic state would cause him to make admissions he wouldn't make normally, he is loathe to expose himself to the complete unconsciousness of hypnosis. The subject must first be convinced that no such self-exposure can take place, since under the influence of hypnosis, no one says or does anything that he would not do, or say under the most normal conditions of consciousness. He must be assured that he will have complete control of himself at all times, and that he will be able to wake up from the hypnosis at any time that he elects to do so.

To avoid difficulty, the hypnotist must shy away from any technical discussion of the somnambulistic state. It is during this state that the subject is under the complete control of the hypnotist, and it is at this time that the subject may reveal content that he would not articulate ordinarily. Should the subject bring this matter up, it is necessary to point out that even though he is in a deep hypnotic state, he will never reveal anything that he does not consciously wish to express. The subject will not, ordinarily, bring this matter up at all, but should he do so, he must be convinced that the technician is not interested in dredging up secrets at all, but rather in helping the patient solve his problems. If the patient has confidence in the hypnotist, he will accept this statement, and they will get on to the matter at hand. "But, Mr. Powers," I can almost hear one of my readers saying, "You are giving the subject false information. You know that in the deepest state of hypnosis, the subject will not remember anything at all!" True indeed! The point is well taken! It is, however, important to remember that we are not at all concerned with the mere by-products of hypnosis, but rather with its benefits. I trust that you have not already forgotten the high ethical principles that were formulated at the beginning of this book. We are ever conscious of our professional integrity, and are not likely to handle any information that may come to us lightly! If the patient is not put wholly at ease, it becomes impossible to hypnotize him. We, therefore, misinform him for his own benefit, since the information that he has repressed, and still does not wish to reveal, may be the very cause of the psychological difficulties. Our attempt to soothe him can be likened to that of the physician who prescribes "Bread Pills" for his patient, knowing full well their lack of worth, but rationalizing his action on the basis of the curative value that the patient chooses to find in them. This, I think, is a fair analogy. We, like physicians, do what we feel is necessary for the well-being of those who have seen fit to turn to us in their need. We, like physicians, employ "Psychological Bread Pills." Our pills, however are made up of reassuring words, that can only be effective if we inspire confidence in our subjects. I think, we are therefore, not only justified, but obliged to employ whatever means we feel necessary for the welfare of our subjects.

The following is such an example of opportunism. I leave it to the reader to decide whether I was justified in proceeding as I did.

Several years ago, a woman, who was afflicted with insomnia, was referred to me. Her physician could find nothing physically wrong with her, and since this condition had continued for several years, without any apparent reason, it was decided that hypnotism might be the means through which the cause of this difficulty might be determined. She was brought to my office, and after introductions, she was prepared for the hypnosis. I instructed her to look at the "Powers Hypnodisc", which I had mounted on my phonograph. Upon seeing this, she chirped, "Aren't you going to use the "swinging locket" that was used to induce hypnosis in the movie, "Road to Rio?" Hypnosis had indeed been used in this moving picture as an aid in purloining jewelry. Having, myself, seen this movie, I was, in truth, very well acquainted with this "locket". Realizing the importance that she placed on this locket, I answered that I had unfortunately left my locket at home, and since I had, we would terminate our meeting until the next day, when I would have the all important locket on hand right here in the office. The lady was satisfied, and we made an appointment for the next morning. When she had gone, I hurriedly sent my secretary out for a locket, after describing the one in the moving picture to her as closely as I could from memory. She came back with one remarkably like my description. I was now prepared for the lady's return, and, in fact, looked forward to it with some anticipation.

She arrived at the office before the time of her appointment, and showed every sign of being excited by the prospect of being hypnotized, "It's just like in the movie," she said, later, breathlessly. I first apologized for my negligence in not having had the locket with me yesterday and we got down to work immediately. I told her that as I counted to three, and swung the locket in front of her, her eyes would become very heavy, and that she would fall into a deep, hypnotic sleep. She was sitting across from me, right in front of my desk, and as I took the locket out of the desk, I could see how fascinated she was by its presence. I counted to three, and within fifteen seconds she was in a deep, hypnotic sleep. I now had her under complete control, and made the appropriate suggestions regarding her insomnia, and the manner in which she could achieve sleep through the use of self-hypnosis. She responded remarkably! She only made three visits to my office, and was soon able to sleep normally again. She was a happy woman once more! It all had been so simple, and only because of her confirmed conviction of the "magic charm" of the "locket".

Here was a clear demonstration of opportunism. Would you have told the lady that there was neither value, nor potency in the locket that she had seen in the movie? Would you have told her that it was nonsense? That any technique would work just as well? Would you have used the hypnodisc, in spite of belief in the locket? My feeling is that it would have been extremely foolish not to have taken full advantage of her faith in the "swinging locket" as I did. She had, already, seen it work in the picture, and, therefore, naively felt it would also work on her. It was all very romantic, but that was the way it was, and I took every advantage of it. The results proved that I had made no mistake at all, and that I had, in fact, made an easy case out of what had previously been a most difficult one, by availing myself of a client's predisposition for a cinematic "swinging locket".

The subject might have been convinced of the efficacy of another method, but wouldn't it have been foolish of me to attempt to divert her when she was already convinced of the "magic" of the "Swinging Locket"?

The good hypnotist takes advantage of every opportunity that a situation affords him, and he deals with that opportunity with such intelligence and insight, that he can almost always be depended upon to achieve the best interests of both his client and himself.

CHAPTER III

You Can Hypnotize Anyone

WE ARE ALMOST all of us susceptible to suggestions in varying degrees, and we are all, therefore, susceptible to the influences of hypnosis. Some react to suggestion very quickly. These persons, of course, make our best hypnotic subjects. They are usually the ones that are used by the stage hypnotists, who delight in their extreme suggestibility. In reading books on hypnotism, you will find that some authors claim to be able to hypnotize only fifty percent of their subjects, while others insist that they are successful with ninety-eight or one hundred percent of their subjects. Why do these authorities vary so much in the percentages of their successes? The answer doubtless is to be found in the nature of the techniques used, or in the practitioners themselves, who may not be activating their medium in the most efficient manner.

What are we to do with those who are seemingly incapable of being hynotized? Are these persons to be dismissed as bad subjects, merely because they are unable to relax or unwilling to cooperate in other ways with the hypnotist? These "problem subjects" can also be made into good subjects through the application of the proper procedure. It has already been proposed that all people are capable of being hypnotized, because of the tremendous power that suggestion wields over our minds and therefore over our actions. I can cite no better example of the suggestibility of the masses than the amazing and effective exploitation of this predisposition by those who are in the advertising field. By repeated suggestions, these people seem able to make us buy anything they wish to sell us. Who of us has not purchased some item, merely because its virtues have been extolled repeatedly to us?

The advertisers' technique must always be kept in mind by the practitioner. The difficult patient must, by repeated suggestion, be "sold" on the idea that he can be hypnotized. If the hypnotist ever makes the mistake of impatiently telling an unresponsive subject that he is difficult to hypnotize, the likelihood is that the technician will never succeed in achieving that end with the subject. No matter how difficult it is to hypnotize a subject, never discourage him, or let him know that you are annoyed with him. Always state that the next time he will go into a deeper hypnosis, and point out that, in fact, no two people react to hypnosis in the same manner, since all people are different. This is indeed a fact. All obstacles to the achievement of hypnosis can be overcome with tact and perseverance.

I like to think of hypnosis as a conditioned response. It can be likened to the conditioning of an animal who is taught to respond to a certain signal. Pavlov's famous experiments with dogs come to mind. Remember how he taught canines to salivate when a light was turned on, since they had been trained to expect food when this occurred? The reflex was so firmly established that the animals salivated at the appearance of light, even when the expected food, which had previously appeared simultaneously with the light, was no longer forthcoming. This is an extremely fine example of a conditioned response, which, once established, becomes automatic in its operation.

This process of stimulus and response is also incorporated into the hypnotic technique. Words have vital meaning to us, because in them lies the power sf suggestion. The words "sleep" and "relax", for instance, convey stimuli to the mind that is totally different from that of the word "fire", for example, if it were shouted in a crowded theatre. It is, therefore, the task of the hypnotist to employ such language and suggestion as to make the induction of hypnosis more certain by the use of only those words (stimuli) that create such feelings of ease and passivity that the response will inevitably be the deep state of hypnosis that is desired by the practitioner.

The success of this operation depends upon the receptivity of the subject. It is my deep conviction, based on my extensive experience, that the subject must inevitably respond to the suggestions of the word stimuli if they are used skillfully by the practitioner. Suggestion is powerful! We have all seen it work! A person in a crowd yawns and before long other people are doing the same. This is a fine example of its power! Try the following experiment on someone: Suggest that you are going to demonstrate the power of suggestion. Tell the participant to think about swallowing, and tell him as he does so he will suddenly have an irresistable urge to contract his throat, even should he attempt to resist it. Now tell him that he will continue swallowing as you speak to him about it. Interestingly enough he will do just that! In fact, this will happen in most instances and is just another graphic example of the power of suggestion. Have you ever noticed how just one person in a crowd who clears his throat, or coughs, can start many others in the crowd doing the same thing? This is extremely interesting, and further evidence of the power of example, and the dynamics of suggestion.

These few illustrations clearly demonstrate how both words and acts can be used as stimuli for the purpose of setting up the proper responses desired by the hypnotist for the induction of hypnosis. Using the proper words, and making the proper suggestions, the technician can set up certain stimulus-response cycles that will insure hypnosis in most persons, because as the previous examples have indicated, most of us are suggestible, and we do react to situations to which we have become sensitized.

Not long ago, a prominent psychiatrist of Los Angeles sent a patient to me to be hypnotized. The psychiatrist had attempted, on many occasions, to induce hypnosis, but had repeatedly met with failure. Since it was imperative that the patient be made receptive to hypnosis, for the needs of further therapy, I was called in on the case, and presented with the facts of the situation. It turned out to be a puzzler, until I found the key to the problem.

In speaking to this patient, I found that his understanding of the science of hypnotism was above average, and that he had no conscious fear of being hypnotized, and yet, despite this, he had still failed to respond favorably to the techniques employed by the psychiatrist. I decided first, that it would be necessary to explore his areas of resistance before I could proceed any further, as my success, of necessity, depended on this information. We discussed his attitude toward hypnosis; the techniques which the psychiatrist had used, the effects that these had had upon him; and his attitude toward himself as a subject for hypnosis. He responded to my questions very favorably, and stated that he had felt some of the effects of the suggestion, however, to a very limited degree. It was established that there had been a good transference between the psychiatrist and patient, which made it all the more baffling. As our discussion continued, I casually leaned over my desk to empty the ash tray, as it had been liberally used by the previous patient, and as I did so, I remarked that he was welcome to smoke as he pleased. He countered by saying that he did not smoke at all, and furthermore, that he did not like the smell of tobacco.

I knew that his doctor was an ardent lover of pipes, and prominently sported a tobacco container on his desk, as well as a pipe stand. I had, in fact, previously conditioned a patient for him in his own office, and had observed him smoking while I was working with the patient. This had never, in my experience, hampered the conditioning process before, and it hadn't on that occasion. Here, however, was a patient who was evidently annoyed by smoking. This, perhaps, might be the reason that the patient did not respond to the doctor's direction, and I suggested this possibility. He thought about it very seriously for a moment, and then replied, "I think you may be right." This reply was just what I had been waiting for. This smoking was undoubtedly the area of resistance that had prevented his complete acceptance of hypnosis. Since he was already acquainted with the hypnotic technique, due to his previous exposure, we went to work immediately. I told him to lie down on the couch, and suggested that he would find himself in a deep hypnotic state by the time the metronome hypnotic record, which I was about to play, had run its course. I further suggested that he listen intently to the beating of the metronome that he would soon hear plainly in the background, and to mentally repeat the word sleep with each beat. I turned on the recording, and after five minutes, took control of the subject, as the recording provided for this shift of hypnotic rapport from itself to me. I tried the "Eye Test", the "Arm Test", the "Hand Test", and a whole battery of other tests. He had, indeed, entered into a deep somnambulistic state! I gave him the suggestion that when his therapist, at some future session counted to three, he would again enter into this same kind of deep hypnotic state. I also conditioned him for self-hypnosis. I called the physician, and told him of my success and the reason for it. He later refrained from smoking while working with this patient. The patient made a reasonably quick recovery, and is well integrated today. Am I always this fortunate with my patients? Of course not! What I am illustrating is merely the importance of checking all clues and circumstances that may throw light on the causes of the patient's resistance to hypnosis.

What is the lesson to be learned by this experience? To me it was a vindication of my contention that anybody can be hypnotized. It is just a matter of finding the technique that will best suit the subject. Areas of resistance can be investigated, and eliminated through patience and ingenuity. It is not always done as easily as I have just related. I have had many trying experiences in my career as a professional hypnotist, but my knowledge and technical experience have usually, however, won the day for me.

Some may argue that smoking was not really the true reason that the psychiatrist's patient was not going under hypnosis. It may be argued that perhaps the subject felt that since I was a professional hypnotist he was more likely to experience the full hypnotic state with me, rather than with his own doctor, who was after all, not a professional hypnotist. Other apparently logical reasons might well be proposed for my success with this patient. Let us assume that my thesis of the tobacco smell is an incorrect one, and that, in reality, this was not at all the reason why the subject did not enter the hypnotic state with his doctor. Perhaps, in my office, some other factor was responsible for my success. These considerations are really redundant, since it was his complete acceptance of my opinion that it was the doctor's smoking that caused the dislocation which proved to be the decisive factor in his achieving the hypnotic state. The patient was convinced that this was his stumbling block, and fully satisfied on this point, he became a splendid subject. The suggestion had worked! That was the only important factor to be considered! That chapter was closed,and it was a good chapter,too, for success had been achieved, in spite of our previous difficulties.

It was the hypnosis that aided in his final cure. Without it, the patient might still be suffering from his malady. I must repeat again, that it is the task of the hypnotist to influence the subject in any way he can to achieve hypnosis. Once these influences are accepted, hypnosis is easily achieved. The patient, having accepted my opinion about the doctor's smoking, saw no further cause for resistance, and proceeded to fall into the hypnotic state with the most encouraging facility. My procedure had worked, and we were both happy about it. I had been vindicated,through my ingenuity, and the patient was closer to his cure. I had made my statement about the smoke so positively and confidently that he had been carried away by my conviction,and had accepted it as fact. He had quickly accepted it, because I had made my suggestion so convincingly that he was infected with it, as it were, and the whole situation terminated, as we already know, very happily for both of us. It was the happy combination of suggestion and the positive psychological approach that had mastered what had been a complicated situation.

The following technique is also an efficient means of achieving hypnosis for those who have proven to be difficult subjects. Most everyone knows that hypnosis can be induced by a swinging pendulum, or by swinging a crystal ball. For those of you who have a pendulum clock, I would suggest the following procedure: Request the subject to sit a few feet away from the clock, and instruct him to concentrate on the pendulum. Tell him, as he watches it sway from side to side, that he is going to fall into a deep, hypnotic sleep. As he does this, suggest to him that it is becoming extremely difficult for him to move his eyes from side to side, and also, that he has but one desire, and that is to fall into a deep sleep. Then, stop for a few minutes, and direct the subject's attention to the problem of concentrating on the project of falling under the influence of hypnosis. Direct him to repeat the word sleep to himself with each swing of the pendulum, which he has been closely observing. You can be sure that this procedure will tire the subject very quickly. He will, thereafter, be ready for deep hypnosis, if he has been dealt with in the proper manner. This technique is also admirably adaptable to self-hypnosis, and can be employed with the fullest assurance that it will be most effective, if properly executed.

CHAPTER IV

Advanced Methods of Hypnotism

IT IS ASSUMED that the reader of this book has had some experience in the practice of hypnosis. It is further taken for granted that he has read some basic book in the field of hypnosis, such as my first book, "Hypnotism Revealed," and is, therefore, familiar with the various tests that are used to determine the various depths of the hypnotic state.

Every book on hypnosis cites the "Eye Test" as being the most efficient means of determining the degree to which a subject is under the influence of hypnosis. This is the method used. After the subject has closed his eyes, seemingly hypnotized, he is challenged to open them. It is suggested to the subject that at the count of three he will find himself unable to open his eyes. Let us say that you have done this, and that the subject, in spite of this suggestion, has opened his eyes. What is to be done? It is quite clear that the subject is not as yet under the influence of hypnosis at all! How do we carry on from this point? Do you petulantly inform the subject that he isn't cooperating, or that he doesn't appear to be a good hypnotic subject? Not at all! Should you do this, you would be handicapped to such a degree that it is likely you would never achieve hypnosis with the subject. It is very likely that some of you have had such disconcerting experiences. To avoid such contingencies in the future, I am going to propose an original technique by which it can be determined whether or not a subject is under hypnosis, without even making him aware of the fact that he is being tested. This method will avoid repetition of the above frustration, and actually make it possible for the hypnotist to be more successful with a greater percentage of his subjects, as this new procedure will tend to keep confidence in him at the highest possible level. Should the response be unsatisfactory, the subject would not have been made at all aware that he had been involved in a technique that had tested the quality of his reaction to the practitioner's hypnotic suggestions. This is no small advantage.

This new technique merely provides that you proceed as you normally would with the subject. Perhaps you have elected to use the "Fascination Method," or perhaps you have directed him to look at the "Powers Hypnotic Crystal Ball" as you prepare to hypnotize him. As you proceed, let us assume that the strain of looking at the crystal ball has caused the subject's eyes to tire and close. The crucial question, now, is, "Is the subject under hypnosis, or is he just resting?" If he is given the direct eye challenge, and he opens his eyes, ground has been lost, for he may feel that he is not a good subject, or worse still, that you are not a good hypnotist, since he had so easily opened his eyes, when he had been challenged to do so. It is at this point, as I have already stated before, that many hypnotists lose their subjects.

It is this impasse that has been the ruin of many a session. To avoid this, after the subject has closed his eyes, continue to give him suggestions that he is in a deep state of relaxation, and that as you (the hypnotist) complete the count of three, he, the subject, will fall deeper and deeper into the ease of the hypnotic state. Begin your procedure. Take a great deal of time before you finally use the "Eye Test." The subject's eyes are now closed. He is in a state of complete immobility and suspension. He is waiting to be commanded and directed. The time for action has arrived. At this point, give the subject the following suggestions: "When I complete the count of three you will open your eyes, and look at the crystal ball. Then, after I give you that suggestion, and when I complete the count of three again, you will fall into a very deep, sound, hypnotic sleep." At another count of three, the subject is directed to open his eyes. Now count to three again while giving him hypnotic suggestions. We know that if he closes his eyes now, that he is under the complete influence of hypnosis. He has followed all instructions. He is in a state of complete suspension.

If the subject has done all as directed (that is, if he has closed his eyes at the count of three,) and if the technician is still not certain of his complete control of his subject, he can still further suggest to him that he (the subject) at the count of three, will open his eyes again, and then close them when he hears the snap of the hypnotist's fingers, since it will now be absolutely impossible for him to keep them open whenever this act is performed by the hypnotist. If there is complete compliance and if the subject's face indicates complete passivity, hypnosis has been achieved.

The practiced hypnotist is able to determine a great deal by the appearance of the patient's face. Others, who are less experienced, will also gain this knowledge in due time. We are now ready to apply all the necessary tests to check the quality of the trance. We know now that they are sure to work, because the previous two tests have been successfully concluded.

You will note that in the suggestions employed by my technique, just described, there was never any mention made of the subject waking at the count of three. He was merely directed to open his eyes. This was done to avoid any possible disturbance of the hypnotic state, which the mere opening of the eyes cannot affect, since it is possible to be in such a state with one's eyes wide open. This also avoids shaking the subject's confidence, by telling him to wake if he had not been asleep in the first place. This procedure tends, therefore, to maintain the high degree of rapport necessary to successful hypnosis. If, in the above example, the subject is under hypnosis, he will, of course, close his eyes immediately at the count of three, or at the snap of the fingers, as directed. The hypnotist would, therefore, have gained his point under the most harmonious circumstances.

There is a question which I am sure must certainly have come to mind, it is: "What if the subject does not close his eyes, after he has been directed to open and close them at the count of three?" What is to be done in this circumstance? This is crucial, indeed! If the subject did not close his eyes, we know that he was not under hypnosis. Therefore, it becomes necessary to proceed, as is normally done, from the very beginning using the same test again, after succeeding in getting the subject to close his eyes. Should the test fail the first time, or even the second, be certain not to show the least sign of annoyance. After a pause, proceed again in a matter of fact and business like manner, so as to insure the fullest cooperation on the part of the subject. It is very important that the subject be made to understand that the failure to close his eyes was not an actual test, but merely a part of the induction procedure. This will insure his continued confidence in the abilities of the technician. I have used this technique with the greatest success. I am certain that you too will recognize its benefits, which are certain to result in a larger percentage of inductions than you have ever had before.

Let us pursue this matter a step further. Let us suppose that in using this technique, we find that we are not succeeding in getting our suggestions across to our subjects. The subject closes his eyes, as usual, but the post-hypnotic suggestion to close them again doesn't seem to have the desired affect. In this circumstance, it will be best to employ another method, or to inform your subject that the next time that you work with him, he will, most surely, go into a deeper state. This is far better than suffering a failure. The subject feels that the difficulty lies merely in the fact he has not as yet been adequately conditioned. This conviction is a much healthier one than the recognition that the hypnosis had been a failure, since he isn't aware that he had been exposed to hypnosis at all. The subject is dismissed, as though this were all a part of the regular procedure, and is not at all aware of what has actually taken place. This method should be used as frequently as possible. It is necessary to repeat again that in the event of a failure, the subject must never become aware of the fact that he has been involved in a hypnotic relationship, because this will handicap the possibility of future success. Merely tell him, that at the next attempt, he will be more responsive. Closely follow the above suggestions, and you will certainly be soon reckoned among those who are classified as successful practitioners in the field of hypnosis.

Here is yet another excellent technique for the induction of hypnosis. Use an ordinary string about a foot in length and tie a finger ring to it. Tie the other end of the string around the middle finger of the subject's right or left hand. It doesn't matter which hand you select. Tell him to extend the hand that has the ring on it stiffly in front of him. The subject is then instructed to close his eyes. After he has done so, he is told that his arm is getting extremely heavy, and that the ring on his hand is getting more and more burdensome, and that as he lowers his arm, which he is told

[42]

is becoming extremely heavy and tired, he will fall into a deep, sound, hypnotic sleep. We are aware that it is a physical impossibility for him to continue keeping his arm in this position for a very long time. Using this knowledge to our advantage, we keep plying him with suggestions that it is the ring that is getting heavier and heavier, thus causing the feeling of heaviness in his arm . As he begins to react to the repeated suggestions, it will be observed that he is gradually lowering his arm. At this point, the original suggestion (that his arm is becoming heavy) is re-enforced, so that the subject is soon under the complete control of the hypnotist. This situation requires the most rapid manipulation of the subject for the surest success, and, if done expertly, is certain to end in his hypnosis.

There is another variation of the use of the ring and string in the induction of hypnosis. It is the "Chevreul's Pendulum Test" for hypnotic susceptibility The same string and ring are used, and in the same manner as before, with the string still attached to the ring. Suggestions are given to the subject, who is invited to close his eyes. As he holds the string, which the weight of the ring has by now made a pendulum, he is immediately given the suggestion that the ring is beginning to revolve in a circle around to the right. Even though he is then directed to hold the string steadily, he has become the dupe of the previous suggestion, and is making wider and wider circular movements with his hand. The subject is then invited to open his eyes. As he does so, he noticed his activity with surprised amazement which soon turns to humor. Such responsiveness denotes the good hypnotic subject. This test can also be performed with the eyes remaining open, but I have found the former method more efficient. This test will be effective with nine out of ten persons. Should it fail, with the one out of the ten, dismiss it lightly by saying, "Now let us go on to the induction of hypnosis." If the subject responds favorably, tell him that he is very susceptible to suggestion, and would make an excellent hypnotic subject. This is the kind of ingenuity and resourcefulness that is the shining hallmark of the successful practitioner in the field of hypnosis.

Chapter V

Eight Original Techniques for Inducing Deep Hypnosis

THIS CHAPTER is going to be devoted to a series of original techniques used in the induction of hypnosis. Like the other techniques, there will be varied reactions from those who are exposed to them. It has already been pointed out on a previous page, that people with good imaginations enter into the hypnotic state with greater ease than others, and that invariably, artists, musicians, writers, and those in other creative fields, having more fertile imaginations, prove to be the best hypnotic projects. There are cogent reasons for this aptitude. The most prominent of which is the fact that those in the creative world find greater accessibility to their subconscious minds by the very nature of their greater, personal sensitivity to internal and external impressions.

Inspiration comes to them through their very pores, as it were, because of their highly attuned sensibilities, and their abilities to withdraw inwardly to the very depths of their being. I am intimately acquainted with a composer, who conceives his most inspirational themes during the night while he is fast asleep. Upon inspiration, he hurriedly awakens, and puts his conception on paper, while the melody still flows richly in his mind. He then goes back to his slumber, satisfied that he has given a beautiful, new, musical score to the world. Many of the famous geniuses of the past have achieved inspiration in the same manner. These artists are the most sensitive of all humans, being much closer than others to the subsconscious realities of their inner selves, which gives them access to thoughts, feelings and ideas that normal people do not even begin to comprehend. This sensibility is both the reason for their genius, and their susceptibility to hypnosis. With such a high order of imagination, they can easily project themselves into a state of hypnosis when requested to do so. When the hypnotist tells such a subject that he is asleep, he quickly assumes that state without the least difficulty. If he is told by the hypnotist that he is to relax, or if it is suggested that his arms or legs are getting tired, he responds automatically. These are, indeed, the finest subjects to be had!

Children also make excellent subjects. The reasons for this become quickly apparent at the slightest reflection on the matter. Children, being what they are, both small and young, are accustomed to being directed by grown-ups. Since they have been conditioned to accepting orders from grown-ups, they accept hypnotic suggestions more easily, and without question. This, added to the lively imaginations that children naturally possess, make them superb subjects. It is most important that the hypnotist remember these facts, since problems come to children, as well as to the more mature, which require the attention of the hypnotist.

Logically enough, soldiers make excellent hypnotic subjects, too, due to the fact that they have been conditioned to obeying orders without question. This is not to say, however, that the method to be adopted with them will be similar to that which is used in the Army. No, of course not! The hypnotist is neither a first sergeant, nor a lieutenant, but a professional man who knows the art of human relationships too well to proceed in the sharp, military manner of the army officer. He will conduct himself with a patient, who also may happen to be a soldier, in the same calm manner, and with the same proficiency with which he treats all other patients, knowing that in this instance, however, he has the advantage of having someone before him who is accustomed to responding to command. In these days of increased military expenditure and a larger army, the hypnotist would do well to keep the soldier, or ex-soldier, in mind as excellent subjects for hypnosis.

If all persons had the hypnotic predisposition of the three above mentioned categories of people; that of artists, children, and soldiers, we would have a vast reservoir of excellent subjects for our research. The job of the hypnotist would then be extremely simple, and the problems would be few and insignficant, but things don't work out quite that way in this best of all possible worlds, so we have to continue to exercise our ingenuity as new problems arise in our day by day preoccupations.

Let us proceed to develop these desirable faculties in our new subjects, if we can. If we are successful in achieving sufficient improvement, both in the areas of the imagination and suggestibility, the induction of hypnosis will be facilitated considerably. This improvement can be achieved through the first technique in the series of my original techniques of hypnosis. This is my first technique: Instruct your subject to close his eyes. Tell him to visualize himself in a classroom, which has a large blackboard in it. Ask him if he has this image in his mind. Most subjects will be able to visualize this picture easily. Tell him to picture himself drawing a large circle on that blackboard. Ask him if he can see this picture in his mind's eye. He will again, probably, say "yes." Then suggest to him that he draw a large "X" in the middle of this circle. Check him once again to see if he is able to retain this image. If he has registered all this in his mind up to now, tell him to erase the complete image from his consciousness. Ask him again if he can visualize the blank circle. If he can do that, you know that you have created a highly suggestible state in the subjec. Now, tell the subject to print a large letter "A" in the middle of the imaginary circle where the "X" had been before. Find out, once again, if he sees this letter in his mind's eye. If he does, tell him to erase it, also, and to substitute the letter "B" for it. Closely note the response. If he has visualized the letter "B", direct him to continue the same process with all the letters of the alphabet, and advise him that when he reaches the end of the alphabet, he will be in a deep state of hypnotic sleep. You continue to make suggestions of deep hypnotic sleep while he is going through the alphabet in the above manner. This technique is very effective. It can be varied by the substitution of numbers for the originally suggested letters, with the identical procedure repeated. You can, in this instance, instruct the subject that as he continues the process of increasing the count, he will find himself going into deeper and deeper hypnosis. This technique, and its variations, are highly effective means of inducing deep hypnosis. The novelty of the procedure, and the fact that the subject has never been exposed to this technique before, is bound to have the desired hypnotic effect.

One of the main difficulties that the hypnotist encounters in his practice is the inability of many of his subjects to concentrate on his suggestions long enough to arrive at the condition of hypnosis. When they are questioned about this, they usually protest that their minds wander, and that they do not seem to be able to do anything about it. This condition is really not unusual, and, in fact, occurs in a majority of instances. Unless the technician makes it a point to prevent this distraction, it is bound to occur. The mind has a tendency to wander, and unless controlled cannot serve the ends of hypnosis! If the subject is diverted, or becomes involved in extraneous matters, he is much too distracted to go under hypnosis. If his mind is completely controlled, however, successful hypnosis is assured. The above blackboard technique is an excellent example of this kind of complete control of the hypnotic subject by the hypnotist. This control is so absolute that successful hypnosis is a foregone conclusion. This control makes access to the subconscious mind an easier matter, since resistance to suggestion has been minimized by the hypnotist's continued direction of the subject's mind and actions. The subject's unrelieved concentration on the hypnotist's suggestions also tends to give him the opportunity to project his imagination so effectively as to strengthen and reinforce the technician's control over him, thus making hypnosis much more certain. The "blackboard technique" is admirably suited to achieve all these advantages, and is, therefore, one of the best techniques available for the subject who finds it difficult to concentrate during the hypnotic session.

This fine technique provides even for those persons who have the lowest attention span. My own experience has proven to me conclusively that they, too, can be made to concentrate through the subtle cleverness of this technique.

The following is another one of the series of my original hypnotic techniques that I have found so remarkably effective in my own experience. The instrument used is a battery pen light. You, no doubt, have seen doctors use them in their practice. Invite the subject to sit down comfortably. You then direct the light from the instrument into one of his eyes, while you tell him to concentrate his gaze upon it, until his eyes become heavy with fatigue. Tell him that at the count of five, he will close his eyes, and fall into a deep hypnotic sleep. Start counting slowly, as you closely note his reaction. If he has not closed his eyes at the count of five, encourage him to do so at his own convenience. Then, suggest to him that he will soon begin noticing a red spot forming inside the one eye that has been exposed to the light. Tell him to look for it, and to inform you immediately upon seeing it. This request is repeated several times to him in a low, soothing voice, until the subject responds to the suggestion. Should he see the red spot immediately, and should he say that he does, tell him that it will disappear in a flash, and that a purple spot will come in its stead. Tell him now that he is to inform you immediately upon observing this purple spot. If he responds positively, that is to say, if he states that he now most certainly sees the purple spot, you can be sure that he can be induced to see most any color you care to suggest, thereafter. It is clear that he is now in such a highly suggestible state, that he can most certainly be brought to the condition of hypnosis. To achieve this, however, the subject must be brought along most carefully. As the subject watches for the change from one color to another, the hypnotist suggests to him that he, (the subject) is very relaxed, and that he will soon be in the hypnotic state. This suggestion is repeated softly, again and again, until it takes effect. The eye test is then administered to check the depth of the hypnosis. This is not the end, however, for to make certain that hypnosis has, indeed, been achieved, further tests should be conducted. If these checks are successful, the subject is definitely hypnotized. The technician can employ whatever technical checks he favors for this purpose.

This is an extremely interesting technique. The hypnosis was brought about, as usual, through psychological means, for the subject was not made aware at all of the fact that it was the continued exposure of his eye to the light that had caused his optic nerve to become so fatigued that he really imagined he did see the spot in his eye that had been suggested to him by the hypnotist. One aspect of the procedure, the eye weariness, was obviously physiological, but the suggestions of the color changes were psychological. Both were responsible for the hypnotic state attained. Subjects are usually very curious about the procedural means employed in this technique. It is the task of the technician to tell his subject only as much as is consistent with his purposes, to avoid difficulty. If, at a later date, he chooses to explain the procedure to the subject, he may do so, without qualms, since his ends have already been achieved. If, however, a student, at any time, requests information on this, or any other technique, he should, for the sake of the student's future efficiency and understanding, be given all of the information available on the subject.

My next technique in the series is an excellent one also. In it, the subject is again completely controlled by the hypnotist. This is how it is done. An hour-glass is placed before the subject, who is seated at a table. He is instructed to watch the sand in the hour-glass as it falls from the upper part of the glass to the lower compartment. It is further suggested to him that as he concentrates on the slow dropping of the sand, he will eventually fall into a deep sleep. To achieve this, however, he must continue to turn the glass downside up, after all the sand has been emptied into the lower part of the receptacle from the upper. This continuous process goes on under a condition of the greatest concentration on the movement of the sand, accompanied by the soft suggestions of the hypnotist that the subject's eyes are becoming very heavy and tired, due to the wearing strain of watching the slow passage of the falling sand for so long a period of time. As he continues to gaze at the slow magic of the falling grains of sand, the suggestions of the hypnotist begin to take its inevitable effect. The subject soon drops into a state of hypnotic sleep, under the expert guidance of the accomplished hypnotist. This technique is one of my most favored ones. It has a romance and beauty that few other techniques achieve.

And now to another exciting technique for the professional or amateur hypnotist. Draw a large circle of dots. The subject is asked to select a dot, and to concentrate his gaze upon it, and as he does so, he is to inhale and say the word "sleep" out loud. He is then to exhale, still looking at the dot, and then proceed to say the words "deep sleep" audibly. While this is going on, and as the subject advances his eyes from one dot to another, still repeating the same formula, he is steadily being exposed to the hypnotic suggestions of the hypnotist, who is soothing him into a deep state of hypnosis. As the subject, however, goes from one dot to the next, he increases the number of inhalations and exhalations, and the repetition of the words "sleep" and "deep sleep," in accordance with the requirements of the technique, so that when he gets to the tenth dot, for example, he has to inhale and exhale ten times, and, also, repeat the word "sleep" and "deep sleep" ten times in the appropriate order as outlined above. By the time the subject has gone through this process for an extended period of time, he has become so fatigued that he does not know where he is, as the saying goes, and, therefore, becomes especially vulnerable to the suggestions of the hypnotist, who tells him that he is now to fall into a deep, hypnotic sleep, which he invariably does, since the hypnotist had already prepared him for this, in advance, by telling him that he would arrive at the hypnotic state during the latter stages of his preoccupation with the "dots".

There is a variation of this technique, which is also a very successful one. The subject is handed a printed page that has nothing but the word "sleep" running through it. As he sounds the word, he uses the same formula as in the previous method, increasing his burden as he goes from left to right, and from line after line, until he, too, becomes so submissive that he, ends up in the same manner as the previous subject. The strength of this technique lies in the fact that the subject sees, as well as repeats the word "sleep" and is, therefore, being assaulted through two of his senses, rather than just that of the hearing sense alone. This, perhaps, tends to make the present technique superior to that of the former one, although they are both admirably effective. This technique has the added advantage of also being useful in combating insomnia. The sufferer is given the post-hypnotic suggestion that whenever a card with the word "sleep" is handed to him, he will immediately fall into a deep sleep. The effects are sure and instantaneous.

And now, we come to another in the series of my original techniques, and, in many ways, one of the most unusual of them all. This technique is one with which my students and I have had the greatest success. Those of you who have read my book "Hypnotism Revealed" will recall that I recommend my first hypnotic record, with its fine musical background, as an effective aid in the induction of hypnosis. This musical background has now been replaced by a metronome, which is even more effective than the music. The subject who listens to the new record is now directed to mentally repeat the word "sleep" with each beat of the metronome. Because he now concentrates on this task, the hypnotic suggestions more quickly penetrate the subconscious, and the subject more readily falls into a deep, hypnotic state. Before this occurs, however, the subject is informed during the playing of the recording, that there will be shift of authority from itself to the next voice heard, which is, of course, that of the hypnotist, who then takes over by saying "When I complete the count of three, you will fall into a deeper sleep. One . . . two . . . . . . three." The hypnotist then makes various checks to establish the condition of the subject.

The same side of the record can also be used for the purpose of self-hypnosis, and in the same manner with the subject, however, instead of the hypnotist, taking over authority at the appropriate time. Most persons enjoy the novelty of listening to a hypnotic record. We, in the field, know that it is a thoroughly tested, and very scientific means of inducing the deep, hypnotic state. All that is required is that the suggestions of the records be carried out faithfully. Most subjects go under hypnosis quickly, merely by listening attentively to the recording, while giving themselves the proper auto-suggestions necessary to achieve this end. By repeated exposure to the recording, the subject, finally, becomes so conditioned to the rhythm of the metronome that hypnosis invariably follows. The metronome hypnotic record was prepared in response to the numerous requests for a new self-hypnotic recording. In this new recording, unlike the original, the musical background has been replaced by the beat of an electric metronome. This creates a greater hypnotic effect than had been heretofore realized by the musical score. One side of the record is devoted to the induction of self-hypnosis; the other, to group or individual hypnosis.

The recording has been so designed as to create the somnambulistic state in the subject, which is known to be the deepest hypnotic state attainable. Twenty years of observation and research have gone into the perfection of this achievement. It is useful for the implementation of self, group and individual hypnosis, and is unmatched in the completeness with which it controls the subject.

Technically, the method is based upon the conditioned reflex theory. The continued beating of the metronome, combined with soothing voice tones, relays suggestions to the listener's ear that bring on the deep hypnotic state.

The recording is made on a 33⅓ rpm unbreakable record and can be played an any phonograph. Should you want the record, send for the Metronome Hypnotic Record. It sells for five dollars postpaid. When ordering, please remit and make checks payable to: Melvin Powers, Dept. E., 12015 Sherman Road, No. Hollywood, California 91605. I sincerely recommend its efficiency to all those interested in the areas of both hetero- and self-hypnosis.

Any of these techniques is an effective instrument in the hands of the skilled hypnotist. The choice, in the last analysis, depends largely upon the specific circumstance surrounding the hypnotic situation, and upon the particular personality of the prospective subject. A resourceful hypnotist always "trims his sails to fit the breeze."

Here, finally, is the last, and somewhat most unconventional of our hypnotic techniques. Hypnotic suggestions are given to a subject while he is normally asleep during the night. In my book, "Mental Power Through Sleep-Suggestion", I discussed the function of the "Pre-Selector Clock", which is a vital part of our "sleep-o-matic unit." You may recall, if you have read this volume, that it can be used both in conjunction with either the phonograph or a tape recorder. Its utility lies in the fact that it will automatically turn these instruments on or off, as fits the needs of the user, and that it can be used during the day, or during the peaceful hours of the night for the purpose of transmitting messages of therapeutic value to the person, who may be either at rest or fast asleep. The clock is set before retiring, and continues for as long a time as is needed to achieve its therapeutic purpose. It then shuts itself off automatically, so that the recipient is not disturbed in the process. Included in the "sleep-o-matic unit" is the "pillow-speaker" which is so placed under the pillow of the subject so that only he gets the benefits of the transmitted recording. This not only improves the quality of the message, but also avoids the possibility of anyone else being disturbed by the transmission. The importance of the "sleep-o-matic unit" is to be found in the fact that it can be used during the hours of sleep, when other media are not available, and also when the subconscious mind can be reached more directly, since the barriers of the conscious state rest quiescentently at this time, and are, therefore, no obstruction to the subconscious mind.

The subconscious mind is the source of our psychic power. It is also the repository of all the repressed emotions which cause so much unhappiness to those who are assailed by them. The "sleep-o-matic units", through the medium of recordings, or through tape transmitted suggestions, can reach the subconscious mind and release that psychic energy that is so necessary to the health and welfare of all persons, and through this liberation makes a new, vigorous and dynamic personality out of a once retarded and impotent individual. This is all accomplished without the subjects conscious awareness of the operation.

There are many persons who have emotional problems, who have neither the time nor the desire to go to a therapist. These are the individuals who would be greatly advantaged by the possession of one of these units, because they could use it in the privacy of their own homes, and at any time they choose without being exposed to, what may seem to them, the embarrassing view of others. For those who feel as these persons do, this unit would be an invaluable possession. I would be pleased to send my readers any information that may be desired on these phenomenal "sleep-o-matic units". My book "Mental Power through Sleep-Suggestion", described on the back cover of this book, contains a detailed account of the use, practicality, and utility of this new technique.

CHAPTER VI

New Procedures for Acquiring Self-Hypnosis

LET US NOW discuss a variety of hypnosis that is both extremely interesting and highly effective, and is commonly known as "Self-Hypnosis". We all know that self-hypnosis comes about through a self-induced hypnotic state, which achieves contact with the subconscious mind through the use of self-suggestion. The need to attain this state is of utmost importance, since through it many psychological problems can be tapped and corrected. The self-hypnotic induction of positive suggestions to the subconscious mind washes away the frustrations that are centered there, and replaces them with vibrant feelings of courage, self-confidence, and self-mastery.

Self-hypnosis, through the medium of self-suggestion, can relieve the pains and fears of childbirth. It is useful in other areas, such as relieving people of such unpleasant habits as nail-biting and smoking, not to mention more major annoyances like insomnia and alcoholism that, unfortunately, plague such a high percentage of our population. Ideas are important, positive ideas or suggestions are more important, but positive suggestions, transferred to the subconscious mind during the self hypnotic state, are most important, since they can cure ills that, otherwise, could neither be solved nor even approached without the subtle influences of self-hypnosis.

There has, up to now, been very little written on the subject of self-hypnosis. In truth, it is only in the last ten years that it has gained popularity, both in the areas of psychotherapy and personal self improvement. I predict, however, that, in the future, there will be an even greater utilization of this medium, which can be so beneficial to mankind. In the early days of hypnosis, the therapist sought to achieve directly the deep somnambulistic state. Starting with Dr. H. Bernheim (1840-1919), however, the founder of the Nancy School of Hypnotism, who was the preceptor of Dr. Sigmund Freud, an exciting new technique was developed. Dr. Bernheim sought first to arrive at the more superficial layers of the lethargic and cataleptic states before attempting to achieve the ultimate state of hypnosis. His success in this made advancement in hypnosis possible. Through this process, results were achieved more deliberately, and more effectively, than ever before, since through this procedure the hypnosis achieved was of a deeper quality than any known before. It was from Dr. Bernheim's experiments that the now famous Dr. Emile Coue developed the practice of auto-suggestion. His famous words, "Day by day, in every way, I am getting better and better," has made his name a household word throughout the Western world, and it is indeed altogether fitting that they should. It is necessary, at this point, I believe, to differentiate between auto-suggestion and auto or self-hypnosis, because they are not at all the same. In self-hypnosis, the subject contacts the subconscious mind, while in auto-suggestion, he does not reach the subconscious mind at all. The advantage of self-hypnosis over auto-suggestion then becomes very apparent. The levels of their effect differ widely; one is superficial, the other is deep. The average person accepts and practices 'the use of positive language daily, not realizing how closely these are allied to the practice of hypnosis. It is also true that we all use auto-suggestion in our daily affairs, without our being at all aware of it. This usage could be set up as an excellent basis for future facility in the science of self-hypnosis, if people only understood that they are indulging in a sort of self-hypnosis most of the time that they go about the daily business of living.

Hypno-therapy and hypno-analysis are rather new developments in the field of psychotherapy. It is within these areas that self-hypnosis makes invaluable contributions to the alleviation of psychological problems. Many psychotherapists do not avail themselves of hypnosis at all, contending that orthodox analysis is the only sure means of arriving at a permanent cure of their patients. Those who deviate from this rigid concept are looked upon with suspicion and distaste. Although the many therapists may admit that much good can be gotten from hypnotism and self-hypnosis, they still hesitate to incorporate them into their therapeutic procedures. It's my conviction, that the basic cause for this is to be found in their lack of understanding of the hypnotic process. Like any other skill, it must be practiced, to be perfected. I have known psychiatrists who had scorned recourse to hypnosis, until they had been prevailed upon to use it for a sufficiently ample period to learn of its efficiency. After developing their skill to a marked degree, however, they tended to use it almost exclusively, as a therapeutic aid. It becomes clear then that the knowledge and practice of hypnosis tends to make it more popular, both with the professional, as well as the lay individual.

The best way to embark on your career as a self-hypnotist is to first have yourself hypnotized, and given the post-hypnotic suggestion that you will be able to achieve the hypnotic state in the future, whenever you elect to do so, by the simple process of counting to three, or by any other means, signal, or a phrase that has been suggested to you by the hypnotist during the hypnotic state. You need only be hypnotized once to make this conditioning permanent, and it is not at all necessary to seek out a professional hypnotist to do this for you, since anyone, who is acquainted with the technique of hypnosis, can prepare the way for you. It can also be done by yourself, if you are sufficiently skilled in the several techniques of self-hypnosis, as outlined in my book "Hypnotism Revealed." There is more information on the subject later in this chapter. It is my urgent suggestion that you try all the techniques proposed so that you can finally select the one which suits you better than any of the others. It is my further suggestion that you set aside fifteen minutes each day for this purpose, for it is the steady application to this project that makes for the best results. Success in self-hypnosis depends largely upon the strength of the conditioning factors. It is well to keep in mind that what we are attempting to do is to set up such a well conditioned stimulus-response cycle,that it is easily activated by a pre-arranged signal which brings about the desired self-hypnotic state. It is the strengthening of this cycle,by constant re-enforcement,that assures the achievement of the hypnotic state.

One of the most successful means of acquiring skill in self-hypnosis is through the medium of our phonograph records. These records induce hypnosis through suggestion. When the subject has been hypnotized, he is informed in the recording that he will be able to hypnotize himself again at the count of three, whenever he chooses to do so. This post-hypnotic suggestion will take effect whenever the subject wants to renew it. Those who cannot avail themselves of a professional hypnotist will find these records extremely useful for the purpose of hypnosis. It is not necessary that these records be purchased from me, or other sources, since you can easily make them yourselves at any local recording studio. A tape recorder, if you have access to one, will also serve this purpose adequately.

My first record was prepared to create a definite,psychological effect on the subject. This was done through means of an appropriate musical background, which soothes and re-assures the listener as it invokes the hypnotic state. Some subjects require only one hearing of the recording, while others require repeated exposure to it. To improve the effect, I recently devised a new recording which utilizes a different approach,altogether.

I now no longer use music, but rather the sound of an electric metronome in the background. This has been indeed a rewarding innovation, because it has greatly facilitated the induction of hypnosis. This idea is based upon the conditioned reflex theory. As the subject listens to the record, it instructs him to pay close attention to every beat of the metronome, and to mentally repeat the word sleep to himself whenever he hears its rhythmic beat. While this goes on, suggestions are also relayed to him that he will be able to hypnotize himself at the count of three. The suggestions usually take effect. I have known subjects who achieved self-hypnosis with this latter recording, but had failed with the former one. I have also observed instances, however, in which the metronome record failed to gain any effect, whatsoever, while the musical hypnotic record was a huge success. People are different. It is, therefore, difficult to tell which record will work. It is best, therefore, to have them both on hand, in case of emergency, so that all contingencies will be provided for.

I shall, at this time, narrate an interesting experience that I had in conditioning a woman who wanted to develop the skill to hypnotize herself. She was highly intelligent, understood the workings of hypnosis, had read extensively on psychological matters, and had a friend who had been relieved of an emotional problem through hypnosis, after all other methods had failed. She told me she had no fear of hypnosis at all, and yet she did not respond to it, somehow. In conditioning her, I used both the metronome record and the electric metronome. I was certain that one of these techniques would work, as the various suggestibility tests had been positive. After several failures, it became evident that there was either some strong subconscious block in her personality, or that my techniques were at fault. I decided that at her next visit, we would investigate her attitude towards hypnosis, since this might tend to further divulge the cause of her resistance. There was, also, the need to check the possibility of a block caused by a fear of expressing herself on matters that she, perhaps, preferred keeping to herself.

When she returned, I found that her attitudes toward hypnosis presented no problem at all, and she also demonstrated an excellent degree of insight into her character and personality. The cause of her resistance, then, had to be looked for elsewhere. In discussing her early childhood, she remarked that the sound of the electric metronome in my office reminded her of the mechanical one she had used when practicing the piano at home, as a child. In pursuing this matter further, I found that she had been forced to practice the piano daily, in spite of her resistance to that instrument. Due to her hostility toward the piano, she made no progress, whatsoever, causing her father much despair and anger. This caused the sensitive child much unhappiness, and she soon quit playing, altogether. The wounds caused by this experience never quite healed. Was this account out of the past the cause of her resistance to hypnosis? It turned out to be so. The sound of the metronome, which she so closely associated with the unpleasant memories of her childhood, caused her, subconsciously, to regress to the unpleasant piano experiences of her early days. Subconsciously, the beat of the metronome in my office, and my position of authority, had caused her to project the feelings of hostility, that had once been reserved for her father, into the present situation. All this had tended to confuse her, and had forced her into a negative mood. We discussed the situation calmly and fully. We decided that the sound of the metronome had been the basic inhibiting factor, and agreed to use the Musical Hypnotic Record, instead.

We, again, proceeded with the hypnosis. She settled herself. I suggested to her that as she listened to the soothing musical background on the record, and as she heard my voice blending in with the hypnotic suggestions, she would fall into a very deep, hypnotic state. She assumed a comfortable sitting position, and closed her eyes when the record started to play. When it was finished, I gave her an eye test, and was elated to find that she was unable to open them. I followed this test with others, which were also successful. We had succeeded at last! This change was all that she had needed to go under hypnosis, and with that successful experience as a base, she soon became an adept student in self-hypnosis.

I have related this incident to you, merely, to show that it is important to investigate every aspect of a person's background whenever a difficult situation presents itself. This same type of analysis should be applied to yourself, should you find that you do not respond favorably to self-hypnosis. The fault may well be within yourself, rather than in the technique employed. For those who desire to develop proficiency in self-hypnosis, I could make no better recommendation than to obtain the record described on pages 56 and 57 of this book. I should be very pleased, should the occasion arise, to lend you whatever technical assistance you may require, if you write to me. After listening to the record, practice its technique without its assistance. This will increase your hypnotic skill. The record itself is to be played daily. This is necessary to develop the proper conditioning for hypnosis. This record, like all records, has two playing sides. Play the self-hypnosis side of the record first, and then play the other side, which is devoted to group hypnosis. Incidentally, the group hypnosis side of the record can be used both for hetero-hypnosis as well as self-hypnosis. One of the suggestions, that is given on this side of the record, is that the next voice heard will take control of the hypnotized subject, after the record has stopped playing. If the group hypnotic side of the record is being used, the self hypnotist takes over at that point, continues the hypnosis, and suggests to himself that the next time he hears the phonograph record, he will fall into a deep, sound hypnotic state, immediately. He, further, suggests to himself that whenever he wishes to hypnotize himself, he has only to complete the count of three, mentally. This completes the process. It is very important to remember that it is urgent that this record be played daily, so that proper conditioning will result.

It is impossible for me, or anyone else for that matter, to state how much time this conditioning will require, since so much depends upon the sincerity of the individual. I have had excellent reports from some persons who insisted that they had acquired sufficient skill to hypnotize themselves with only one playing of the record. Others have written me insisting that they had been compelled to play the record about fifty times before they finally achieved the desired results. Those who are suggestible will, naturally, be conditioned much more quickly than those who are not. Remember, however, that anybody can learn who is sufficiently conscientious and interested in the project! It is only a matter of being conditioned correctly.

Here is another exciting technique which you can use to acquire skill in the science of self-hypnosis. After you have gotten into bed, and turned off the lights, do the following: Give yourself the suggestions to relax, just as you would ordinarily give them to any subject you were about to hypnotize. In this case, however, you direct the suggestions to yourself by using the pronoun "I", since this is the procedure in self-hypnosis. When you feel that you are sufficiently relaxed, and are about ready to fall asleep, give yourself the following suggestions: "When I mentally complete the count of three, I shall fall into a deep, sound, hypnotic sleep, and direct constructive suggestions to my subconscious." You, then, mentally complete the count of three, while you improve the quality of your relaxation by the appropriate suggestions between each number counted. As you reach the count of three, you will feel a decided physiological change come over you as you approach a state of contented relaxation. Having arrived at this condition, give yourself whatever mental suggestions you think fit. When you have done this, give yourself the post-hypnotic suggestion that the next time you complete the count of three, you will fall into a deep, sound, hypnotic state at once. When first using this technique, you may not feel that you are actually in the hypnotic state at all when you have finished the count of three, but in spite of that, continue to give yourself hypnotic suggestions, and also the post-hypnotic suggestions, so that you will eventually find yourself in an even deeper state the next time you perform the count. It is by this process that a deep hypnotic state can be achieved. The full effects of it will be observed and appreciated by the more conscientious pupil, who is bound to achieve success in the field of hypnosis, if he continues to apply himself intelligently.

In carrying through the preceding technique, it is essential that it be carried out to the very letter. After the count of three, as I have mentioned above, many feel that they are not in the hypnotic state at all, since they are still aware of what is going on about them. In self-hypnosis, this is truly the case, because the person remains very aware of his own suggestions, and furthermore must be sufficiently conscious of himself to direct them to his subconscious mind where they will take effect. It is only in the deep somnambulistic state that the subject is not aware of what is going on about him at all, so that he even fails to recall what had taken place during the induction of hypnosis. The advantage of practicing this technique prior to going to sleep is that we are most relaxed at that time, and since we are, we are much closer to achieving the subconscious condition that plays such an important role in the process of hypnosis. We are thus taking advantage of a natural condition to achieve our ends. It is interesting to note that we pass through the hypnotic state before falling into a state of natural sleep. Our purpose then is to use this understanding as a means of facilitating and insuring the ends of hypnosis. Suggestions during this relaxed period find easy access to the subconscious, because the resistance of the conscious mind, at this time, is very low. As I have mentioned elsewhere, the subconscious mind begins to take control when the conscious mind lies in a state of dormancy. Because of this, suggestions have access to the subconscious mind, making this period the best suited for self-hypnosis.

Many persons have the ability to solve problems while they sleep, and wake up with solutions they could not possibly have achieved in their more conscious moments. The statement "Let me sleep on it" is commonplace to all of us. In this announcement, we are unwittingly admitting the power of the subconscious faculty without realizing it. The moments just before sleep then are the best time for the achievement of self-hypnosis, because we are then so much closer to the subconscious source of our power, that we can tap its hidden resources with the greatest ease.

ADVANCED TECHNIQUES OF HYPNOSIS

I have often been asked by an anxious student how long it would take him to acquire sufficient skill to hypnotize himself. It was, of course, as impossible for me to answer that question as it would be for me to be able to forecast how long it would take a person to learn how to type at the rate of fifty words a minute, drive an automobile, or to play a musical instrument. I am sure, however, that given the proper instruction and time, anyone can learn to do any of the above activities in a reasonably short time; just as anyone can learn how to use the hypnotic technique skillfully, if given the proper training and opportunity. I have found that most persons can acquire skill in hypnosis within a two week period. In my own courses, I find that five lessons are usually all it requires to achieve this end. I have known some students who needed but one session to acquire this facility. These persons, however, are, obviously, unusual, while others may not be able to acquire this skill until their twelfth visit. This wide disparity is quite interesting, and is one of the intriguing problems of hypnotism. If a technique could be devised which would work with equal effect upon all persons, it would be of great service to our work, and to society as a whole. It would mark a great advancement in the field of psychotherapy. Interestingly enough, most students who come to our school from out of town acquire hypnotic skill rather quickly. Very few of these pupils have failed to achieve the highest proficiency and technical skill in the hypnotic techniques while attending our classes. Since our course lasts but for a limited time, and since these students have sometimes traveled great distances to attend my school, they get down to work very quickly and very soon are finished practitioners in all phases of hypnosis, because of their deep interest and great industry. It is,obviously,this type of student who makes my work rich and satisfying, and leaves me with the warm feeling that I am making a constructive contribution to our social welfare.

I have, in the previous pages, mentioned some of my successes. I would like now to relate one of my failures. It was,at least,a partial failure. A young man had traveled to Los Angeles from Texas for the purpose of learning self-hypnosis from me. I tutored him for a full week. He attended our group lessons, and had an opportunity to observe how the other students acquired skill and knowledge in the field of hypnosis, and yet was himself unable to achieve the slightest results. It was disappointing! Was I,somehow,at fault? Had I unwittingly,overlooked some important factor? If I had, I certainly was not aware of it. He was keenly disappointed, and I was at a complete loss to understand the cause of the difficulty. I advised the student to continue listening to the hypnotic record every day, and also to practice the technique of self-hypnosis before going to bed. He had followed my injunctions during the whole period of his stay, but had derived no benefits from them,whatsoever. He made ready to leave, but reluctantly promised at my request to continue his conditioning at home, and to report his progress to me at the end of the two week period. He wrote to me two weeks later, informing me that he had shown some improvement in his hypnotic conditioning, but that he had as yet, not achieved the self-hypnotic state. I wrote to him suggesting that he continue to apply himself, and to again, let me know how he was getting on at the end of another two week period. It was only a week later that I received an excited long distance telephone call from him, informing me that he had finally conditioned himself to self-hypnosis. My suggestions had finally worked, but only after he had left my personal supervision. I was convinced that there had been an area of resistance that I had been unable to pierce, while he was under my direction, which had proved to be an insuperable obstacle in our path. This was, of course, not a complete failure, since he had finally achieved his goal, but I consider that I had failed him in some way, that I have even as yet not been able to determine. His perseverance had finally paid off! I heard from him once, several years after he had made his appearance in my office. He was still very happy about his skill as a hypnotist, and was very pleased that he had been my student, in spite of our difficulty.

I suppose, that I should logically not have mentioned the above experience, since I am writing a book on hypnotism and since I am considered an expert in this field, but we all have our failures, and I am no exception to the rule. The sea, after all, is not always smooth. I have had the occasion to condition many subjects on their first visit, even though it had been their intention to stay a full week or more with me. I think it is necessary to present all kinds of experiences, so that the reader will have a fuller understanding of the complexities of hypnosis. Regardless of the proficiency of the hypnotist, difficulties do arise, because people are different and present diverse problems.

Very often, the student, in his first visit, is more interested in the techniques of self-hypnosis, than in the self-hypnosis itself. It is, of course, understandable for those individuals who have read on the subject, or have had a previous interest in it, but what of those who have no previous knowledge of the subject? They obviously need a background in hypnosis before we can proceed with the techniques, and we supply it to them. Most classes are more or less alike, no matter what the field of study. Some in the class will develop their skills quickly, while others will require a great deal of time. Some soon lead all the rest; others seem to just tag along. However, in the long run, most of them learn. Keep this fact well in mind, whether you teach others, or if you are just a beginner, yourself. If you have trouble learning at first, do not become discouraged. You will gain this skill if you give it the proper attention and application. Everybody does, who is sincerely interested in this fascinating field. It is well worth both the time and energy it requires.

Let us now discuss some further techniques. Those of you, who are cinema fans, may recall the picture "Whirlpool", which showed in many of our theatres throughout the country several years ago. The scene is a hospital. Jose Ferrer has been taken back to his room after a very serious operation. He is in severe pain, and to relieve himself of this torture, he decides to hypnotize himself using a hand mirror to do so. He is soon relieved of his gnawing pain through its use. The hand mirror is an excellent means of achieving self-hypnosis, and that is the only reason I cited its use by Ferrer in this moving picture. I recommend its use to the reader as an excellent technique for the induction of hypnosis. Take a small mirror yourself and hold it before you. Look into it and give yourself the suggestions that your eyes are becoming tired and very heavy. As your eyes become heavy and watery, re-enforce the suggestion of heaviness. Then,proceed to give yourself the suggestion that as soon as you close your eyes,you will fall into a deep, sound, hypnotic state, but that you will, however, still maintain your ability to give yourself whatever post-hypnotic suggestions you desire. This is a wonderfull, effective technique. Try it. I am sure that you will find the results very gratifying.

In my book "Hypnotism Revealed", I discussed the use of the "Powers Hypnodisc" as a means of achieving self-hypnosis. You will, no doubt, recall that the hypnodisc is placed on a revolving phonograph turntable, and as it revolves, hypnotic suggestions are given by the subject,to himself while his eyes are concentrated upon the whirling center of the hypnodisc. This technique has always been extremely fruitful. A variation of this technique is to stand the hypnodisc upright, against a supporting object. As the subject looks at it, he imagines that the disc is beginning to revolve to the right. When this image has taken full hold of his imagination, a suggestible state has been achieved. The subject is now well on his way. He now pictures the disc to be revolving to the left. When this has been successfully imagined, he gives himself the final suggestion that he is to fall into the hypnotic state.

The self suggestion is phrased in the following manner: "When I complete the count of three, I shall enter into a very deep, hypnotic state, and will be able to direct suggestions to my subconscious mind." This will invariably be achieved under the proper conditions. I have included a picture of the hypnodisc in this book. It can be used as a substitute for the original disc. Those of you who desire the genuine twelve inch "Hypnodisc", can get it through my office at the very nominal price of one dollar.

Let us now pass on to yet another method for the induction of self-hypnosis. Here is how it goes: Lie down and close your eyes. Try to visualize a very pleasant scene. Think of yourself as actually there. If it is difficult at first, do not become annoyed. Try again. Once the image firmly takes hold, a heightened sense of suggestibility has been achieved which can be utilized as a means of inducing self-hypnosis. This method is also an excellent one. I enthusiastically recommend it for your use.

Let us keep the following facts in mind as we go about our tasks: Hypnosis is defined as a highly suggestible state of mind. Our job in hetero and self-hypnosis is to establish this highly suggestible state, and to use it as a means of implanting the proper suggestions. The hypnotist, in trying to establish this tractable state, might suggest to the subject that he picture himself as floating on a cloud, or as lying in a hay stack, in a state of perfect calm and contentment. This will tend to create the proper hypnotic mood in the subject. If the hypnotist can capture the imagination of his subject sufficiently, hypnosis is assured. The subject must, himself, learn to use his imagination in achieving self-hypnosis. That is the reason, a fact we have already established, that the artistically inclined make good subjects. They have the enviable ability to project themselves, in such a manner, as to make themselves the best hypnotic subjects.

Most people are fond of music. This love of music can, also, be used for purposes of self-hypnosis. If records are carefully selected, with an ear for their soft and soothing effects, such great benefits of relaxation can be obtained from them that they can be used most admirably in paving the way to the final goal of the self-hypnotic state. Music is a simple and pleasant aid, and easy to come by what with phonographs, radios and television available in most homes. Music has definite physiological effects upon the nervous system. It is, therefore, necessary to get the proper type for hypnotic induction since only soft, peaceful tones can pacify the prospective human organism. This, then, is the kind of music I recommend, both for hypnosis and therapy, for none other will do. I have special musical records containing very relaxing piano music, which I especially advocate for these purposes.

I have just finished writing a book dealing exclusively with self-hypnosis. This book contains all the information that is known about self-hypnosis. We approach the subject from many different viewpoints that will be of extreme interest to the serious student. The ultimate goal of the book is to give the reader knowledge of himself, his resources, and his potentialities.

To this end, I have written the book titled, "Self-Hypnosis, Its Theory, Technique and Application." It is one that will require careful reading and studying. It is written, primarily, for the advanced student of hypnosis, with the hope that it will lead him to still greater heights in his personal development. It is hoped that the book will, also, serve as a stepping-stone in awakening a keen interest in many related subjects. The book is further described on the back cover of this book.

CHAPTER VII

Waking Hypnosis

WE ARE ALL AFFECTED by the irresistible influence of suggestion. We merely vary in the degree to which we respond to it. By systematic suggestions, multitudes can be made,through propaganda,to act as a unit, even though there had been no previous attachment to the ideas communicated. Under the stress of emotional stimuli, we are led easily to commit acts that we normally would never dream of perpetrating. The protagonists of propaganda know this well, and,thereby,exercise their power to create conditions that will make their assault on the public mind more successful. Political agitators, also being aware of mass susceptibilities, work on this disposition for their own purposes, thus demonstrating that such entities as individuals, groups, and nations can all be made to act in a manner that suggests the influence of hypnosis. This effect is most notably achieved through the irresistible force of suggestion,rationalized under the most properly prepared conditions,for their greatest effect.

Our commu predisposition to suggestion is also manipulated by the hypnotist, who also first prepares the subject, but under totally different conditions from that of the propagandist or agitator. The hypnotist invites feelings of calm, while the former flourish on rank emotionalism. All distracting emotional stimuli and ideas are cast aside by the hypnotist while the subject listens to his placid, soothing suggestions, which soon cast a spell of peace over him. In this situation, all external stimuli, such as light and sound, are minimized to the greatest possible degree, so that the peace of relaxation and sleep can be attained more quickly. The suggestions of the hypnotist bring passivity and the hypnotic state; the thermal stimuli of the war propagandist, or political agitator bring rancor and frenzy. The instrumentality is the same, but the goals are as widely diverse as hysteria and slumber, and are, of course, intended to be so.

People are effected by many kinds of stimuli. Examples of this are numerous in our everyday activities. A mother puts her child to sleep by singing and repeating the lulling words "Sleep my child, sleep my child"; a man sitting in the barber's chair listens to the sound of the vibrator, and as he concentrates upon its humming monotone falls asleep; others fall asleep listening to the soft tones of music coming from the radio; while many, who search for physical beauty, find themselves asleep under the relaxing balm of the beautician's touch. In each of these circumstances, sleep had only come, because all other distractions had been so effectively eliminated from the consciousness of these persons that the one dominant stimulus in the environment was bound to effect the passive listener. This information should serve to give us a better understanding of the conditions favorable to "Waking Hypnosis", which we are about to discuss. Let us first proceed with some particularly fine examples of "Waking Hypnosis".

A nurse recently told me of a patient who came to the office, in which she was employed, for the purpose of getting an electric diathermy treatment for an ailing shoulder. The patient was directed to lie down; the diathermy unit was applied; and the nurse left him to attend to her other duties. She returned after a time, turned off the machine, and asked the patient how he felt. "I feel so much better", he said. He dressed and soon departed. When the nurse later prepared to go home, she made the usual check of the office to make certain that everything was in good order, and much to her surprise and amusement, noticed that the diathermy plug was not in the socket. In fact, she now reflected, she had failed to insert it back into the socket after sweeping the floor that morning. She had been called to the telephone as she was about to do so, thinking that she would attend to it after she had finished speaking on the phone. But other things had intervened, however, and she soon forgot about the whole affair.

"The heat had helped my shoulder so much," he had declared, and "the unit hadn't even been on," she chuckled. This is an extremely good example of "Waking Hypnosis," with all the elements present to make it a classic illustration.

Here is another instance of "Waking Hypnosis": A friend of mine, an extremely eminent physician, told me that out of sheer curiosity he, sometimes, when applying an antiseptic solution, which never burns, tells the patient that it is going to sting momentarily, and sure enough, he responds as though it had! He, also, at times, says he gives his more hypochondriacal patients a bitter, harmless medicine, telling them that it is an extremely sweet and pleasant one to take. He notes, quite frequently he insists, that some of them will, on occasions, actually smack their lips with pleasure after swallowing the bitter stuff, sometimes even sighing, with regret, that the dosage was so small. This is an extreme case, of course, but it has happened, he insists. The human mind accepts what it is prepared to accept, and even when it doesn't materialize, behaves as though it had, merely because it has been conditioned, through suggestion, to anticipate it. Thus, we have the phenomenon of "Waking Hypnosis."

One of the best demonstrations of "Waking Hypnosis" is the following test that you can use with a group. It is usually the one that is employed by the stage hypnotist for the purpose of choosing those of his audience who will make the best hypnotic subjects. Request the members of the group to clasp their hands together. Tell them at the outset that this is being done merely to determine which of them has the best aptitude for concentration. Have them clasp their hands together and squeeze them gradually tighter. Inform them that at the count of three, they will find it impossible to unclasp their hands, no matter how strenuously they may attempt to do so, until they are instructed to do so by yourself. There will always be, in any average crowd, a fair percentage of those present who will not be able to undo their hands until they are directed to do so by yourself. They are the ones that you can control! Note them! They are your best hypnotic subjects! The interesting point in all this, however, is the fact that these people are awake and, in spite of it, you have succeeded in contacting their subconscious minds, thus completely controlling them.

What is the element here that makes this an extraordinary good example of "Waking Hypnosis"? It is merely the fact that these persons are being controlled solely through the suggestion that they would be absolutely unable to unclasp their hands under any condition whatsoever, and the added feature is that they had responded as though this were actually the case. This is a clear example of a situation that seemed real only because suggestion had made it so. "Waking Hypnosis" is a powerful instrument of control, and should be used by the hypnotist at the proper time to expedite hypnosis. Its use in everyday life is widespread.

The techniques of hypnosis have gained greater popularity than ever in the field of business and advertising. Recently, the head of one of the nation's largest breweries took a course in hypnosis with me. He was interested, primarily, he said, in the use of suggestion. He learned of its potency through my instruction, and later put it to expert use, both in his private life and his business adverising. He wrote the advertisements himself, using the principles of suggestion in such an efficient manner as to increase the sales of his product voluminously. That suggestion has been used in advertising is an old story, but that hypnotic techniques have been added to it, is new and sensational news! It has now become a commonplace to see these techniques used in television advertising. I suggest you observe some of the television advertising this evening. Notice how closely they apply the methods of hypnosis, and note how effective the advertising is, as a result. I have been asked, on several occasions, by members of advertising agencies what they could do to incorporate the principles of hypnosis into their client's advertising copy. I invited them to take my course. They did, and were well rewarded for it, for their success was swift and phenomenal! Their business improved, due to their greater insight into the mass mind, and their greater understanding of the techniques of suggestion.

I, myself, bought a new hair preparation recently that had been advertised on a television program. I was not at all impressed with it when I saw it, at first. But, after being constantly exposed to its view for a protracted period, I finally succumbed to the suggestions of its efficiency, and so sauntered down to the corner drug store to purchase a bottle of it. I actually was not in need of a new hair tonic at all, for I was moderately pleased with the brand that I had been using, but the repeated suggestions, that this new brand was much better than the others, made such an impression upon me, and, no doubt, upon the others in the television audience, that I, like the others, succumbed to the repetitious insistence that "There had never been a hair tonic like this made before." It turned out to be an excellent hair tonic, indeed, but that is hardly the point with which I am concerned here, since my primary reason for citing this experience was to indicate how exhaustively the power of suggestion controls us wherever we may turn, and to point out that the average person's predisposition toward suggestion can be channeled to the purposes of "Waking Hypnosis".

There is a variation of the "Swallowing Test" that has not been discussed as yet in this book. This one is used in "Waking Hypnosis". Here is how it is used: Suggest that the subject think of the act of swallowing. Tell him that if he does so, he will find it impossible not to go through with it, even though he may try to resist it. Tell him that should he try to resist it, he will feel a great sense of unease. To avoid this sense of anxiety, the subject will invariably respond as directed, since he desires to maintain his sense of well-being. This is another graphic example of the force of "Waking Hypnosis".

"Waking Hypnosis" has been used, for many years, by doctors who utilize hypnosis. We find reference to this interesting technique in the book, "Suggestion" by George C. Pitzer, M.D., who published his book in the year 1898. He cites the use of this technique under the section heading "Suggestion for Cure in the Waking State," and has much to say on this vital technique that is of the utmost interest and importance to those who are interested in this area of hypnosis. He writes, "A lady came to me suffering from a severe neuralgia of the face. She told me that she had heard of the wonderful healing power of animal magnetism (hypnosis) and wanted to be exposed to it. She described her ailment in detail, was in great earnest, and confidently expected relief. I listened very attentively to all she said. I felt at once that I could cure her; I had no doubts at all about a cure. In fact, I felt that I knew I could cure her. While she remained seated, I arose and approached her with a firm and earnest expression on my face, and with an air of confidence, I took her right hand in mine, and placed my left hand upon the painful part of her face. I then requested her to close her eyes, and to keep them closed while I spoke to her. I addressed her in this fashion: "Madam, the position of our hands, one of mine holding one of yours, while the other is fixed upon the painful part of your face, will immediately change the nerve current in your body. You will soon feel this influence all over you. You are beginning to feel it already. The nervous forces in your body are seeking, and will soon reach, conditions of equilibrium. It is already coming. An easy, quiet feeling is coming all over you. Your whole nervous system is easy and quiet. You feel easy and quiet all over. The pain will soon leave your face, and it will feel perfectly easy. A proper distribution of the nervous forces will completely relieve all of the pain in your face. It is already coming, coming, and your face is feeling better. Your face feels warm now, and the pain is rapidly disappearing; it is going away, going away, your face feels only warm now, and the pain is going away, going away; gone, all gone, all gone, and your face feels warm and comfortable. Your face feels warm and comfortable; the pain is all gone. You feel quiet and easy all over, and your face feels perfectly easy, and you feel well all over your body—perfectly well." I then repeated the above formula, with slight variations, several times, still keeping my hands in place. This patient, from the start, had believed in the efficacy of the treatment, I felt that she had confidence in it, and she obtained complete relief at once. She had heard of the wonderful power of animal magnetism (hypnosis). This had served as a forcible suggestion, and she was already, therefore, prepared for good results. I had observed that her desires and expectations were positive. This had put both of us at our ease, and by both our outward expressions our mutual feeling were realized by one another, both objectively and subjectively. We fixed her attention, and then simply suggested, by our behavior, gestures and spoken words together the changes and conditions we wished for. Her subjective mind took cognizance of the suggestions without any questions, and the desired results were fully realized. The time occupied was about fifteen minutes. I instructed her to frequently repeat to herself the suggestions I had made to her, those being: 'The pain is all gone, all gone. My face feels comfortable and warm, etc.' I call this friendly auto-suggestion. It prevents relapses. I also requested her to say nothing about the treatment to anybody for a week or two, but to say to people, who might inquire about her health, that she is well and happy."

This is a marvelous example of the most spectacular

activation of the dynamics of "Waking Hypnosis" and illustrates how effective its power can be when the proper conditions prevail for its successful application.

A well-known dentist, who took my course in hypnotism, told me of the very interesting use he had made of the "Waking Hypnosis" procedure on one occasion. Instead, he said, of giving one of his patients a shot of novocain as a local anaesthetic, he showed him a wad of cotton, saying that he was going to saturate it with novocain, and apply it to the area from which the tooth was to be extracted. He made a great display of placing the cotton into the solution that the patient thought was novocain, but which was, in reality, just plain water, and then placed the cotton into his mouth, with the reassuring words that the patient's gum would soon be numb. The patient was invited to inform the doctor whenever he felt his gum sufficiently frozen to permit the extraction of the tooth. The patient, surprisingly enough, responded as though he actually was under the effects of novocain, and the doctor proceeded to extract the tooth without the slightest discomfort to the patient. This was "Waking Hypnosis" indeed!

Another one of my students, also a dentist, told one of my classes in hypnosis about a fascinating experience he had had with one of his patients. The patient was to have a tooth extracted, and, being very fearful of the experience, requested an anaesthetic. The doctor asked him whether he would accept nitrous oxide gas. The patient said that he would, and that he, in fact, preferred that anaesthetic to all others. The nasal mask was placed over his face, and he was instructed to breathe deeply. He was very soon in a deep state of unconsciousness. His tooth was extracted. He was brought back to the normal state, and shown the tooth that had been extracted. He was then told by the dentist that although the process of placing the mask on his face had been executed, no gas had been permitted to run through the tubes. He had thus had the operation performed without an anaesthetic. The patient was surprised, then embarrassed, and broke into a sheepish smile as he realized that he had been a guinea pig in an interesting psychological experiment. The doctor added, with a twinkle in his eye that the patient had been his own son. He stated, however, that he had since tried it on others, and that it had worked just as well. "Waking Hypnosis" is an extremely effective technique, as the two previous dramatic experiments have so amply demonstrated. It is the task of the hypnotist to use it whenever the occasion warrants it.

The successful hypnotist is a masterful psychologist, besides being an efficient craftsman. He knows life, people, and society, and always observes these with an eye toward improving his skill and understanding, so that he can make a greater contribution to the welfare of his fellow men by helping them solve their mental, physical, and emotional problems. Professional men of all fields can utilize the benefits of "Waking Hypnosis", but it is the student of hypnosis, and those professionals in the field of hypnotism, who must lead the way, because of their greater intellectual and technical understandings of its subtle technique.

CHAPTER VIII

Secrets of the Stage Hypnotist

THE STAGE HYPNOTIST has always been a source of keen interest to the public, and has frequently fired its imagination with his sensational showmanship. While the stage hypnotist's activities do seem to be histrionic and magical to the uninitiated, the students of the subject know very well that his procedure is extremely scientific, and carefully calculated to gain his ends. Let us sit in on a session in which the stage hypnotist is already at work, and notice how scientific his approach really is.

The subject is seated upon the stage. He has already volunteered and has been accepted. The hypnotist turns to him, and either commands him in soft, convincing tones to fall into a deep, sound, hypnotic state, or merely to fall into a normal state of "sleep". The subject complies, in a manner that reminds one of an automaton, which, having no will of its own, performs its task in an automatic manner. Why this amazingly rapid response? Does the hypnotist possess some strange magic? No, obviously not! He is just an expert technician who knows what he is about, and has literally set the stage for his success, which was assured from the start, because of his ingenious procedure. The reader is already not only aware that all people are suggestible, but that they are not so to the same degree. The hypnotist never forgets this fact for even a moment, and bases his entire procedure upon this understanding. He also has another advantage which has been carefully prepared, even before he makes the request for a volunteer to come upon the stage to be the subject for the stage demonstration of hypnosis. The technician has meanwhile been gradually building up his "prestige" with the audience by his professional manner and self assurance, so that by the time he finally asks for a volunteer, it has already been generally accepted that he is an expert in the field of hypnosis.

The hypnotist has, in the meantime, however, taken the precaution to give the audience a group hypnotism test, and through this has become acquainted with those members of the audience who are the most suggestible of the persons assembled. He selects a volunteer from among this group, and his success is thus assured. The reputable hypnotist never uses a "plant". He is far too efficient to resort to such pettifoggery, since his knowledge and proficiency in the science of hypnosis is so well grounded that he is always assured of success in his undertaking. Furthermore, the effect of the hypnosis on the audience is far greater when one of the familiar members of it volunteers to be a subject. This always lends an interest and excitement to the occasion, which would otherwise be lacking. I have arrived at this conclusion on the basis of my vast experiences with such audiences all over the country. For example, when I had my own television show in Hollywood, I always made it a point to have new persons appear on my program from week to week. This not only increased the entertainment value of the program, but also gave it an air of authenticity that it otherwise would have lacked.

The audience is almost always aware of the reputation of the stage hypnotist. That is the reason people come to see him perform. The audience assumes that the man is an expert, and comes to see him perform a practical demonstration of his skill. It is, therefore, already disposed in his favor, thus constituting itself as a suggestible unit to be manipulated by him. The hypnotist comes on the stage, greets the audience in a friendly and professional manner, and informs them that an interesting experience is in store for them if they will but sit back and relax. He gives them a short lecture on the history and purpose of hypnosis, thus creating an air of greater interest and understanding of the hypnotic science, thereby enhancing their suspense and vulnerability more than ever. He pursues the matter further by stating that since the audience is united by the common bond of its great interest in hypnosis, excess talk and other distractions should be held to a bare minimum. In this manner, the path has been smoothed; interest has been heightened; expectancy has been raised; a common bond has been created; and a unified motivation for hypnosis has been achieved.

The hypnotist now proceeds to inquire whether there are any persons in the audience who talk in their sleep. Since a common audience rapport has already been created, its members do not hesitate to respond at all to this question. We thus find admissions being made that ordinarily are suppressed. This high sense of co-operation is further evidence, that the group is well disposed both toward the hypnotist and the hypnotic experience itself. As the question is asked, the hypnotist raises his own hand to indicate that he wants those who talk in their sleep to do likewise. He carefully takes notice of those who raised their hands, registering these persons in his mind; and then invites them now to lower them again. He now requests those persons to raise their hands who have successfully responded to the "Ouija Board". After these have done so, and have also lowered their hands, but not before being observed and noted by the hypnotist, he asks for a show of hands from those, who have had their handwriting analyzed, or fortunes told. He again mentally registers those who have responded to his questions. The most important question, however, is yet to come, and that is a show of hands from those who have been previously hypnotized. These are the ones that the hypnotist has been looking for, for they are the most suggestible persons in the audience, along with the others who had responded to his former questions. This group was the final object of his search. He is now prepared to proceed with the project of selecting a volunteer from this suggestible group. He has proceeded cleverly. The reason for this procedure has been two-fold. The audience had not only been made attentive to the requests of the hypnotist, but those members of the audience, who were the most suggestible and, therefore, the best potential subjects, had been made known to the hypnotist without the audience realizing what had been going on.

Having already determined those who would make the best subjects, and having, at the same time, gotten the audience under his control, the hypnotist now states that the best subjects were those who had raised their hands in response to his request, but quickly adds that the others could become equally good subjects if they followed his directions most carefully.

He now proceeds to test the hypnotic susceptibility of the group as a whole through the use of the "Hand Clasp Test". He invites the whole audience to participate in this exercise which he states will test their combined abilities of concentration and relaxation. He sets the example for this by extending his arms stiffly before him, and interlocking his hands as he does so. The audience is invited to do the same, and having assumed this position, they are directed to squeeze their hands very tightly, while they look into the eyes of the hypnotist. While this is going on, complete silence is requested to avoid the slightest distraction in the procedure, since the fullest concentration is required. After the audience has complied with the hypnotist's suggestion, he announces that the members of the audience will now be unable to separate their hands, because these are now permanently locked together. He keeps repeating this suggestion with convincing insistence. They are told that the more they attempt to pull their hands apart, the closer they will cleave together. This is deliberately repeated with calm conviction, and as the hypnotist continues to turn his gaze upon the audience, he informs them that at the count of three, not one person will be able to pull his hands apart. He proceeds to count to three, stating that now their hands are inseparably bound together, and will be so, until he chooses to release them. He maintains that the harder they try to divorce one hand from another, the more frozen they will become. He continues to repeat this, as his eyes wander about the room checking which ones in the audience were still unable to unclasp their hands. He cautions the audience to remain silent to avoid disturbing those whose hands remain frozen.

There are usually persons in the audience who are, indeed, unable to unclasp their hands. They sit there in rigid amazement, while the "unfrozen" members of the audience look upon them with mixed feelings of shock, surprise, and amusement. The audience is again cautioned to remain silent, while the "frozen ones" are directed to stand up. After they have risen to their feet, they are informed that at the count of three, they will be unable to keep their eyes open, and that they will fall into a deep, hypnotic sleep. The numbers are counted, all eyes are closed, and they are now under the complete control of the hypnotist. In this phase of the procedure, it is necessary for the hypnotist to speed up his suggestions, so that the subjects will fall into the hypnotic state more quickly. This avoids the possible dislocation of the hypnotic process. In the next phase, the subjects are told that they will open their eyes at the count of three, but that they will not awaken from the hypnotic sleep. They are then instructed to go onto the stage, and to take seats there. (It is important for the reader to notice that while the subjects' eyes are opened, they are still under the influence of hypnosis.) They are further told that when they get to their seats on the stage, their hands will become unclasped, and that they will again close their eyes, and fall into a deeper hypnotic sleep than they experienced before. The stage has now been set for the actual demonstration, for the subjects are now under the absolute control of the hypnotist. The stage hypnotist has arrived at this point, not by prestidigitation, but by a considered scientific approach to the problem of hypnosis. It becomes clear then that he is not a faker, but a serious technician.

The hand clasp procedure should not take more than five minutes. This method can be employed either with one person, or with a group consisting of hundreds of people. It must have become apparent to the reader, since he has now sat in on a session of stage hypnotism, that there is nothing mystical about the hypnotic procedure at all, but that it is an expertly conceived operation based upon the findings of psychology and hypnosis. This clever technician took each step with calculated care and purpose, and as he brought his audience along, through intelligent direction and keen insight, he knew that he could not miss achieving his purpose. Not only because he knew his business, but because he was very responsive to, and highly conscious of, the people with whom he was working, was he able to keep them under perfect and masterful direction at all times.

There is yet another technique that can be used successfully by the stage hypnotist for group hypnosis. The audience is informed that a group hypnotic record is going to be played for their benefit. They are further told that if they listen closely enough, it will bring about a state of hypnosis in all of them. This excellent hypnotic record is the "Metronome Hypnotic Record", which is fully described on pages 56 and 57 of this book. It is also an excellent means of inducing hypnosis. It is, in fact, the best recording of its type. I say this with authority, since I have done much research in this area.

As the record plays, it suggests that when it is finished, attention from it (the record) will be shifted to the next voice that is heard. The voice, of course, will be that of the hypnotist, who takes over as soon as the record is finished. The hypnotist then immediately continues where the recording left off, by giving the audience further suggestions of deep, hypnotic sleep. He then administers the "Eye Test" to probe the effect of the suggestions. He does this by counting up to three slowly, saying that at the end of the third count, it will be impossible for the audience to open their eyes, no matter how energetically they may try. Those who are unable to do so are, of course, under the spell of hypnosis. They are requested to raise their hands. When they have complied with this request, they are told that they will find it impossible to lower their arms when the count of three is completed. Those who are unable to do so are in a cataleptic state. The technician can proceed as he sees fit from that point; instructing the subject to comply with all post-hypnotic suggestions. This technique is one of the easiest and quickest means of achieving mass-hypnosis.

Either one, of the two techniques described, in the present chapter can be used as the hypnotist sees fit. They are both excellent means of inducing group-hypnosis, and merely await the animating touch of the hypnotist's skill.

Chapter IX

How "Instantaneous Hypnosis" Is Accomplished

ONE OF THE MOST interesting aspects of hypnosis is the phenomenon of "Instantaneous Hypnosis." I have been requested to divulge the mystery of this phenomenon on numerous occasions. When I answer that there is no mystery in this procedure at all, but that it comes about solely through the skillful application of psychology, I am met with incredulous stares. The fact of the matter is, nevertheless, that the operation is quite simple, and requires but an understanding of applied psychology, and skill in the manipulation of hypnotic suggestion. "Instantaneous Hypnosis" is indeed, a sensational, but nevertheless sound, hypnotic phenomenon.

The following is a fine example of it: In the book, "Hypnotism" the author, Dr. George Estabrooks, relates an extremely interesting experience. I refer those who want a more detailed description of this event to page thirty-eight of this fascinating volume. The doctor had called a group together to conduct an experiment in hypnosis. He informed the group that he was going to play a hypnotic record, and that this record was to cause them all to fall into an immediate state of hypnosis. In selecting the record, however, the doctor mistakenly placed one on the turntable that was not a hypnotic record at all, but was rather a Swiss yodeling song. As he hurriedly got up to correct his error, by replacing this record with the proper one, he chanced to glance at one member of the group, who had instantaneously fallen into a hypnotic sleep as the record had started to play, in spite of the fact that no hypnotic suggestions had come from the record at all, since, as I have explained already, the wrong recording had been placed on the phonograph. As a result of this experience, this highly intelligent and experienced hypnotist realized that it was not necessarily the technique that was crucial in hypnosis, but rather the faith and prestige that the technician can arouse in his subject in the pre-hypnotic phase of the procedure. This experience had resulted in a state of "Instantaneous Hypnosis." Despite the fact, that the proper recording had not been played at all, merely because the doctor's fame, as an excellent psychologist and technician, had built up the proper state of suggestibility in the affected person. Now, it is perfectly true, that only one member of a group had been put into a hypnotic state. That cannot be denied, but this experience proved invaluable to the doctor, since it made him realize the vaulting importance of the pre-hypnotic phase of his operation. He took full advantage of this accidental experience, and before long, became exceedingly adept at the practice of inducing "Instantaneous Hypnosis." It is no small comfort, to those in the field, to have had an illustrious person, like Dr. Estabrooks, verify the importance and success of "Instantaneous Hypnosis."

In my experience, I have found that most persons are brought more quickly under the influence of hypnosis when they are part of a group, than when they are alone. For the past ten years, I have conducted many hypnotic group sessions. This extended series of experiences has convinced me that this is certainly so. In my group course, my first purpose is to condition the class to self-hypnosis. In order to achieve this end, I must first use one of them as a model subject, and before I proceed to hypnotize him, or her, as the case may be, I stress the need of the class to closely observe the physical reactions of the person going under hypnosis. While this model subject is under the state of hypnosis, I ask minute questions about his condition and feelings, and how these differ from the pre-hypnotic state. The answers are closely noted by both the class and myself, and are exhaustively analyzed through a detailed discussion of every phase of the experience. Through this pragmatic procedure, the students learn all about the hypnotic state, and its related manifestations. When this pilot demonstration and discussion are finished, the other members of the class are not only anxious to be hypnotized, but know analytically what to expect, and how to react. Such an advantage can only be achieved through a group seminar. The students are soon very highly learned in all facets of hypnosis, after having first learned how to hypnotize themselves. These are the persons who become the most vulnerable to "Instantaneous Hypnosis" because of their great interest in it, and because of their previous pre-conditioning, which makes them so pliant to suggestion, that the merest mention of hypnosis often forces them under its immediate control.

Here is yet another instance of a case of "Instantaneous Hypnosis", resulting from a previous interest in hypnosis and a very high regard for the prestige and status of a hypnotist, who had travelled four hundred miles to give a personal demonstration of the science of hypnotism to an interested group.

Several years ago, I was invited to come to San Francisco for a speaking engagement. After my lecture, I was importuned by the president to attend a reception in his honor that was to be given at his home. He suggested that since it was still early, (the lecture had been given at the conclusion of a Saturday luncheon,) and since I had come directly to the lecture from Los Angeles, that I go home with him to rest and freshen up before the reception that evening. I was invited to partake of a light repast with his family, which consisted only of Mr. Howard, his wife, and his son, William, a bright young student of eighteen, who was attending the university at Berkeley, just across the bay from San Francisco.

William seemed very impressed with my profession, and confided to me that he had received some very excellent reports on the virtuosity of my demonstration at the luncheon that afternoon. He told me that he was extremely interested in hypnosis, and that it had, on several occasions, been discussed with great animation, in his abnormal psychology class at the university. He went on telling me about his interest, and finally looked at me rather uncertainly and blurted out the words: "Would you consider hypnotizing me?" "Of course, I would, if you would enjoy it," I replied. He responded with tingling excitement to the prospect of being hypnotized, and we proceeded under the interested eyes of his parents.

Before we started, I asked William to get my case, which I had left in the guest room upstairs. He went up for it like a flash; came back almost before we realized he had been gone; placed it at my feet; and asked me what he must do now. I told him to shift the chair closer to me, then sit down and relax. He responded to my suggestions immediately, and there he was before me, awaiting my next proposal.

I took a "Hypnotic Crystal Ball" out of my case; held it before him with my finger tips; told him to relax; and to concentrate on its shiny surface. I told him that I was going to utter the word "Sleep" three times, and that he he would close his eyes, and fall into a deep, hypnotic sleep at the third mention of that word. He did so immediately. I quickly gave him the "Eye Test", and found that he was absolutely unable to open his eyes. I tried several other tests with the same results. He was assuredly an Instant Hypnotic Subject. When I returned him to the conscious state again, he asked me all sorts of questions as to what he had said, if anything, during his unconscious state. We all assured him that he had distinguished himself in every way in his responses, and then we all had a good laugh and sat down again to have dinner, as William regaled us with his remarks about learning how to become a bona-fide hypnotist himself.

Having read this account, you could very well inquire why the hypnosis had taken such immediate effect without any previous conditioning. The answer is clear enough. William had developed an interest in hypnosis during the discussions of the subject in his abnormal psychology class at school. His interest in the subject had been further deepened by his own reading. These facts, coupled with the circumstance of my coming such a long distance to give a lecture before his father's club; plus the fact that he, at last, had a real, live, professional practitioner visiting at his home; and finally his ever present desire to be hypnotized, which he had never had satisfied due to his lack of opportunity; all made him a preeminently good subject for "Instantaneous Hypnosis."

The truth is, that with William, I need not even have gone to the trouble of using the hypnotic crystal ball at all since his predisposition to hypnosis was so great that he actually succeeded in achieving this condition through the pull of his own highly charged self-suggestion. He had been the best subject imaginable!

A test, that is frequently used in producing the instantaneous hypnosis state, is the "Falling Back Test." In this test, the subject is asked to cooperate with the hypnotist for the purpose of determining the extent of his proneness to "Instantaneous Hypnosis." He is told that if the test is successfully completed, he will forthwith fall into a state of hypnosis, and will thus have proven himself to be a good subject. He is further assured that this is the standard test for this purpose. The subject is instructed to stand erect, to place his feet together, and to close his eyes. At this point the hypnotist tilts his head a bit, purposely, to set him off balance. The subject is not aware that it will have that effect. The hypnotist then places his hands on the subject's shoulders, as he stands behind him. The subject is then instructed to imagine that he is falling back. He is told that as he does so, he will be prevented from hitting the floor by the hypnotist, who will break his fall, and that he need therefore not have any fear on this account. The subject is also advised that he is to sway himself at the ankles, as though they were made of hinges. The hypnotist rocks the subject slightly backward and forward to illustrate his point, and finally brings him, to what the subject thinks, is the normal upright position, but which actually is not so, because he has been brought back beyond the point of perpendicularity, which, of course, the subject doesn't know. The subject is now in an off balance position though he does not realize it. He is again given the suggestion to think of himself as falling back, and as this suggestion is given, the hypnotist gradually releases the pressure of his hands from the shoulders of the subject, and so of course, the subject falls back as a result. The subject is now very pleased with himself, because he feels that this is conclusive proof that he has a high sense of susceptibility to suggestion. The subject is told that he possesses excellent control over his mind, and that he, also, has a fine imagination, or he would not have responded so admirably to the hypnotist's suggestions. Now, he is told, he is ready for hypnosis. The subject is then seated, and the hypnotist immediately proceeds to induce the hypnosis. The subject is told that at the count of three, he will be unable to keep his eyes open, and that he will immediately fall into a deep hypnotic sleep. This will surely take effect if the hypnotist observes the normal principles of hypnosis, and applies them expertly. This technique is one of the finest known to hypnotic science. I, therefore, recommend it heartily.

I cannot stress too much the importance of creating a feeling of confidence and good rapport in any prospective subject. He must, unalterably, be made to feel the competence of the hypnotist, for without that confidence, nothing can be achieved. If, in the course of a hypnotic session, the subject does not enter into the state of hypnosis immediately as desired, the hypnotist must lightly remark that this situation will be corrected at the next session.

I have a special technique for those subjects who tell me that they had failed to go under hypnosis before, or for those who feel that they are going to be very difficult to hypnotize. I ask these persons whether they have ever heard of hypnosis being induced by drugs. The answer is, usually, in the affirmative, since this kind of information usually reaches the public through such media as the novel, or the moving pictures, or perhaps through the reports of medical journals, which often cite the extensive use of sodium amytal and sodium pentothol as cortical depressants. Upon learning that they have some knowledge of the use of these drugs, I inquire whether there would be any objections to swallowing "A Hypnotic Pill", composed of the above compounds, which aids in the establishment of a deep state of hypnosis. Should the subject consent, I extract a placebo (which in this instance is a sugar coated pill that has no value at all) from an impressive appearing medical container, and give it to the subject, along with an ordinary glass of water. I tell him that the reaction to the pill will be instantaneous, and that he will soon feel very drowsy. I tell him, further, that upon taking the pill, his eyes will quickly become very heavy, and that as he closes them, he will fall into a deep hypnotic sleep. He has no sooner taken the pill when I, immediately, suggest that he is feeling very drowsy. The usual response is that this feeling, actually, does overcome the subject, who is soon in a deep hypnotic sleep.

Any harmless pill would have made an equally resourceful placebo. "Instantaneous Hypnosis" has, therefore, been achieved through the mere application of elementary psychology. The subject's confidence in my authority as a hypnotist had made him accept my word without question. The acceptance of a useless pill as the real article came about only because the patient believed in my ability as a practitioner of hypnosis, and because I was careful to maintain in my relationship with him such a high degree of self-assurance and efficiency that the warmest rapport with him became inevitable. Hypnosis is, in the last analysis, not

only a matter of technique, but also one of personal relationship, which is, perhaps, the more important of the
two.

I assume that the reader is familiar with the nature
of the post-hypnotic suggestion, which can also be used
effectively in "Instantaneous Hypnosis." I will, therefore, not elaborate on it at this point, as I have already
done so in my book, "Hypnotism Revealed." The rule,
that should be always remembered,regarding "Instantaneous Hypnosis" is that, once the subject has been
hypnotized, he can be put into that state again,imme-
diately,by being given the same signal, key word, or
phrase that had been originally directed to him when
he was under the hypnotic influence before. When the
same key word,or phrase,is uttered, the subject falls into
the same hypnotic state as previously. It is not within
his power to resist these key words at all. This is,ob-
viously,the best and surest manner of inducing the state
of "Instantaneous Hypnosis", since the way has already
been prepared for it,in advance,through the post-
hypnotic suggestion that the subject respond to the same
stimulus as before. This latter method of hypnosis should
be used as often as possible, not only because of its
economy of time, but because it minimizes the possibility
of external distractions that so often hamper the smooth
flow of the hypnotic procedure.

Chapter X

Hypnotic Techniques in Psychotherapy

IT IS NECESSARY, AGAIN, despite the fact that it has been detailed before, to mention the importance of the practitioner's manner in his administration of hypnosis. Should the procedure falter at the first attempt, a situation that comes to pass very frequently, the technician must continue his work as though nothing at all amiss had occurred. Patients, who have been referred to me by others in the field, have often told me how disappointed their practitioners had been when they had not responded well at the first hypnotic session. No wonder these sessions had been failures! The hypnotic situation is an extremely sensitive one. The least discordant note, therefore, is bound to disrupt the calm and balance essential to the successful conclusion of the hypnotic induction. These hypnotists, had by their attitudes, both consciously and unconsciously, prepared the way for their failure.

I, too, feel a sense of disappointment when I experience failure, but when I do, I don't blame the subject, nor do I show the least evidence of distemper. I merely proceed again, knowing, from my not inconsiderable experience, that all subjects are not alike, and that I must, again, repeat the procedure with greater care and deliberation, so that I will be better able to detect the flaw in the operation that had caused my failure. If, in rechecking my procedure, I notice nothing faulty in it, I will return to another technique, which will be more amenable to the subject's personality and temperament. The personal equation is the most important single factor in the hypnotic situation! That fact must never be forgotten! The following account of a veteran's experience will illustrate this point graphically.

A veteran, of World War II, was being treated psychiatrically by one of the most prominent psychiatrists in the city of Los Angeles. Our government, in appreciation of the veteran's sense of duty, and his great sacrifice during the last war, had granted him a pension so that he could live in some comfort, while he was being cured of his disability, which he had suffered in a battle. He was being treated by a psychiatrist so that he could, again, regain his pre-war sense of personal worth and emotional balance. As the veteran had turned out to be a "difficult" case, hypnosis was attempted, since other means had failed to pierce the strong mental and emotional blocks that he had set up between himself and the world. As the psychiartist was not an accomplished hypnotist, he had failed, completely, to pierce this "wall", and, so, had referred the case to me for further investigation.

In taking up the hypnosis where the doctor had left off, I found the patient had been sufficiently orientated to it, and, in fact, was anxious to "go under", since he had read much about its therapeutic value. He insisted that he was not at all reluctant to go under hypnosis, and that it was erroneous of me to suggest that he was. Checking closely, I came to the conclusion that everything had been done that should have been done in pre-conditioning the patient, but the results, however, remained negative. Yet, had the therapist really done everything that could have been done? He must have failed somewhere, or else defeat would not have resulted. Something must have been overlooked! What it was, I didn't know. I, a professional hypnotist, had been called in on the case. It was my responsibility to find the clue that had caused this "block", so I could help cure this unfortunate fellow. I decided to proceed carefully, hoping in this way, to unearth some small sign that would help me in this puzzling case.

We sat down to talk in the calm atmosphere of my inner office. I offered him a cigarette. He graciously refused,stating that he had never smoked. I asked him whether he objected to my smoking. He said he didn't. I got up to get an ash tray,and sat down again, sliding back into the deep, comfortable recesses of my favorite chair. We,now, sat facing one another, both of us relaxed and at ease.

As I smoked lazily, exhaling circles of smoke that formed and diffused even as they took shape, he started to talk about his youth, which had been spent in a small, mid-western town; of the death of his younger brother, whom he had loved so much; of the divorce of his parents, when he was but thirteen years of age; of the remarriage of his mother to a "good for nothing", who had mistreated her; and of his own precipitated departure to New York City,at the age of seventeen, where he had gotten a job as a waiter in a restaurant and had courted cloying loneliness, until he had met a wonderful girl.

Here is the story he told me of his romance, which I am almost compelled to relate because of the wonderful light that came into his eyes when he started to relate it to me: "It was a rainy, unpleasant night," he said. "I was twenty years old at the time. I had just walked out of a theatre, thinking that I would take the street car on the next corner. It had been raining hard all day, the streets were slippery, and as I turned, I noticed the lithe, lovely form of a rather tall girl, who was walking hurriedly a short distance ahead of me. As I had just come out of the picture show, I was filled with feelings of romance and idly thought that it would be pretty wonderful to know a girl like that, and quickly dismissed her from my mind.

"As I walked rapidly, forgetting the fast moving figure ahead of me, I suddenly heard a shriek and saw the girl teetering wildly, as she flailed her arms to prevent herself from falling on the treacherous sidewalk. Her efforts failed, however, and as I ran up to aid her, I noticed that she had fallen in such a manner as to have twisted her ankle. I chanced to be the only person around who had witnessed the incident. I asked her whether she was badly hurt. She said she didn't think so, but as she attempted to stand, she moaned with pain. Her ankle had taken a bad turn in the fall. I summoned a taxi, and saw her home. We became warm friends. She later became my wife. I went into the restaurant business soon after my marriage, and made a success of it. I was very happy, until the war came when I decided to enlist, and do my part to protect our country." And here he was, now, just a shell of a man. It was his great love for his wife, and little boy, he said, that made him so unhappy to have returned to civilian life in the shattered condition in which he found himself.

He told me about his war experiences. He narrated the story of his basic training; of his shipment overseas; of his first experience of terror in active combat; of the death, misery and destruction of the battlefields; of his being in the Italian Campaign where the American army had been caught under the merciless fire of the murderous German gunners; of his being taken from the battle-scarred area of combat, because of a wound; and of his eventual "breakdown" in the army hospital in Rome to which he had been sent, and from which he was, eventually, returned to the United States.

It was the stress of battle and his painful wound, he said, that had caused him to crack up. It had become too much for him to handle, and he had become unconscious. As he spoke of his war experience, he trembled with visible fear. I suggested to him that he, perhaps, should discontinue speaking of it, as it seemed to unnerve him. He said it did not disturb him as much as it had in the past, but that the terror of it still hung on. He continued to speak and seemed to cover every aspect of his war experiences, but that of his being wounded. He seemed, somehow, not to want to talk about it, and when I pointed that out to him, he became visibly agitated. I veered the conversation away to other matters, and he soon relaxed, again. As we talked on, I suggested to him, casually, that I had read of a case of a man who had exposed himself to unnecessary danger during combat, and had, as a result, been wounded. As a result of this wound he had been sent back to the rear for medical treatment, and had suffered an emotional breakdown. I eyed him carefully, but unobtrusively, as I mentioned this. He perspired visibly. I pursued the matter further saying:

"It was found later, through hypnosis and psychoanalysis, that he was suffering from a sense of guilt as a result of having exposed himself unnecessarily to enemy fire, hoping he would get hit and so be sent to the rear. When the case was cleared, and it was found, through repeated sessions, that the soldier had not exposed himself unnecessarily at all, but that he had, in fact, saved a gun position, he exclaimed, 'But I thought of doing it on numerous occasions.' It was pointed out to him that what he had done was natural enough, since his instinct of self-preservation was merely at work, at the time, as it is in all of us, in time of danger. It took a long time, but he was finally convinced he was not a coward," I said, ending the story as I looked closely at him sitting there in an agitated condition.

As I was narrating this story I noticed a great fidgeting in his behavior which had become more marked as I continued. He finally burst out with a torrent of words, which tumbled out with such rapidity and hysteria that all I could gather from the whole content were the disconnected words: "I didn't want to get hit! I didn't want to get hit!" His voice cracked with the tension of this outburst, and he sat there, before me, with his face in his hands, sobbing convulsively in despair and terror.

After his crying had subsided, and when he had regained some degree of composure, I calmly lit another cigarette, and sat back and asked him whether he had ever told the psychiatrist the circumstances under which he had been wounded. He said he hadn't. He had been too frightened and embarrassed to bring it up. We had at last found the cause of the psychological block! I asked him more about the circumstances of his having been wounded. He hesitated for a moment, and then perhaps because of my sympathetic manner, told me the particulars:

"The enemy's fire was particularly heavy at the time," he narrated. "It was being used as a cover to protect the movements of a detail that had been sent out on a scouting foray. As we returned the fire with equal intensity, I noticed that the man next to me had been hit before he could get into his foxhole. He was lying there bleeding from a severe head wound. I got out of my hole, and as I crawled in his direction I was found by an enemy bullet." This obviously had been an act of heroism, but because of fatigue and nervousness, and because of his secret desire to get back to the rear, he could never be sure whether his purpose was one of altruism or sheer cowardice. This had complicated his emotional life and had contributed to his breakdown.

This young man was eventually cured. His insistence that he was not afraid of hypnosis was not true. His fear that he would expose himself was too great for him to overcome. He consciously wanted to "go under" thinking that it would help him, but his subconscious barriers were too great to achieve this end.

I asked him how it came about that he had divulged his secret to me, while he had not done so with his psychiatrist, whose training in the field of deep therapy was, after all, much greater than mine. He told me that it was the coincidence of my story, in which I had presented a crisis similar to his own. Needless to say, this "coincidence" was not one at all, but rather a hunch that had come out of my observations of the patient. The psychiatrist, who had sent him to me was an extremely competent doctor, but even he, as brilliant as he was, could only work with a patient that would cooperate with him. This the patient had been unable to do, because of his fear and shame.

The patient did not go under hypnosis until after several visits with me. His subconscious resistance to it had to be gradually eliminated through sympathetic attention, and technical manipulation. How far could I have gotten with him, had I shown the least annoyance in my treatment of him? Obviously no where! But success came at last, because he went back to his doctor with the proper frame of mind to insure his cure.

Our first two visits were confined mainly to friendly conversations, in which we took every opportunity to get to know one another better. Our relationship was cordial, but not by any means intimate, because while it was necessary for the patient to develop confidence in me, it was also necessary for me to retain his high respect, for to be effective, a hypnotist must retain his prestige for the surest success.

I brought him along gradually, taking one step at a time. It was not until his fourth visit that I finally attempted an "Eye Closure". I did not try any further tests; merely informing the subject that we would proceed further the next time, and that he certainly would feel much more disposed to hypnosis than ever before. It took him a little deeper in his next visit. On the visit after that, he asked me if I were going to use the "Hypnodisc" in the induction of hypnosis, since I had mentioned it frequently in our previous conversations. Up to that time, he had been somewhat passive, but friendly, during our conversations, only answering questions when asked to do so, and rarely ever taking the lead in the conversations. Since he had reached such a state of congeniality, I felt that it was the psychological moment for me to move rapidly. I told him that he was now ready for deep hypnosis, and that the hypnodisc he had inquired about would be used to induce this state. I turned on the portable phonograph that had been tilted upright for easier vision, and directed him to concentrate his attention on the hypnodisc, which was now rotating on it. I told him that when he felt he was being drawn into the center of the hypnodisc cone, which effect the whirling spiral produces, he would immediately fall into a deep, hypnotic state. In a few moments, his eyes closed and I knew then that we had accomplished our task. All the hypnotic tests were positive. He had entered into a deep somnambulistic state. While he was in this state, I gave him the suggestion that his doctor, the psychiatrist, would be able to put him into this same state whenever he counted to three in his presence. I also suggested to him that all would be well for him in the future.

This all seemed so simple now that our purpose had been accomplished, but it had been a case that had taxed all the ingenuity at my command. I was rightly pleased with the results. Patience, skill, delicacy, insight, and imagination had all made their contribution to the success of this complex situation. As I look back at that experience now, I realize that it was a "perfect case", because it had taxed me to the fullest, and because it had required a synthesis of all that anyone ever need know about hypnosis, and the art of dealing with people. Dr. Theodor Reik, the renowned psychoanalyst, was perfectly correct when he stated in his splendid book "Listening With The Third Ear," that the expert therapist develops a sixth sense. We know, that those of us who function in the field of hypnosis, have developed this sixth sense as an essential tool of hypnosis, which is certainly one of the most interesting sciences in the world, and one that can bring great healing benefits to mankind.

Readers, who want to further develop their skill in hypnosis would do well to read the various books that are outlined on the back cover of this book.

CHAPTER XI

Hypnotism Does Help

HYPNOSIS HAS COME OF AGE! It is now accepted seriously by those in the field of medicine, as well as others whose work it is to help people in need. The following articles are but a small demonstration of the increased respect which this science enjoys today. The intelligent reader will gain much information and insight from them, and will, perhaps, be encouraged to take a greater interest in the work that is yet to be done in this field.

The following article appeared in the September 1, 1952 issue of TIME:

ENTRANCED SKIN

When he was born, in London, even his mother thought that he seemed to have a thick skin. As the baby grew, his skin darkened and hardened to a black, rough casing over his whole body except the chest, neck and face. It was covered with close-set black bumps; between them the skin was as hard as a fingernail, and if it was bent it cracked and oozed blood-stained serum. Someone cruelly dubbed him "the elephant boy." Doctors said he had been born with ichthyosis (fish-scale disease). Nobody knew its cause or cure.

Treatment at some of London's best hospitals did no good. A trial operation to graft normal skin from his chest to his horny palms proved worse than useless: the grafted skin blackened like the rest, then shrank and stiffened his fingers. The boy went to school, but his teachers and other pupils objected to him. Though he was quick to respond to affection, he got so little that he became shy and lonely.

Then Dr. Albert Abraham Mason heard of the case. In his studies of psychosomatic conditions, he had taken an interest in hypnosis. Eighteen months ago, in a white-painted hospital room in East Grinstead, Sussex, a dozen skeptical doctors watched as Dr. Mason talked the boy into a hypnotic trance. It took ten minutes. Then Hypnotherapist Mason said again and again: "Your left arm will clear." (He had begun with a particular part of the body to make the test more precise.)

About five days later, the coarse outer layer on the boy's left arm became soft and crumbly, and fell off. The skin underneath was reddened, but soon became pink and soft. In ten days the arm was clear from shoulder to wrist.

Dr. Mason tried again and again, cutting his hypnosis time to three seconds. After he said the right arm would clear, it did. The boy's thighs and legs, which had been most heavily covered, cleared partially. His back was 90% cleared. The boy, now 18 and happier than he had ever expected to be, has learned to hypnotize himself to maintain the improvement. He is working as an electrician's helper.

Skin specialists who read of the case last week in the staid **British Medical Journal** snorted, did not see how hypnosis could ease a condition which began in the womb. Neither could young (26) Dr. Mason, but he had witnesses to the treatment and the boy's improvement.

HYPNOSIS CAN BE GREAT AID TO MEDICINE

LONDON.—Make no mistake about it, hypnotism is a matter of vital importance, affecting nearly everyone. Statistics show that 80 to 90 per cent of people can be hypnotized, and can derive benefit from its use for a wide variety of ailments.

Hypnotism can help in cases of asthma, migraine, duodenal ulcers, blood pressure, skin diseases, allergies, hysteria, neurasthenia and insomnia. By the use of hypnosis more and more women are bearing children without feeling the slightest pain, and there even is a case on record of a woman being cured of warts by hypnotic suggestion after months of medical and X-ray treatments had failed.

When we consider that a wart, which is only a growth, can be made to disappear by suggestion, we are entitled to ask: May we be able to influence other growths? It is only a possibility, and only years of painstaking work, experiments and research can supply the answer.

Let me hasten to explain that hypnotism is not a cure-all for human ills. It can be used in widely varying conditions, and nobody, no matter how fanatically opposed to hypnotism, can deny that in this science we have the most powerful and effective method of controlling the mind and, through the mind, the whole body.

When a few words, suggesting paralysis, can make a hypnotized person powerless to move, though fully conscious and able to reason, who can doubt the power of hypnotism? When hypnotic suggestion can cause the mouth to water, change the heart rate, or cause sweat glands to function, who can fail to be impressed with its possibilities in medicine?

Hypnosis may be regarded as the key to the mind of man. Neuroses, illusions, delusions, and hallucinations can be induced experimentally under hypnosis, and as quickly removed.

Surely such a powerful weapon must be of the utmost importance in investigating the cause of mental disorders.

Fortunately there are signs that the medical world is beginning to realize the immense potentialities of the science which, stripped of all its nonsensical and mysterious trappings, can be presented as a simple, serious and straightforward method of medical treatment. Hypnosis, after all, is proving to be of immense value in the treatment of many diseases.

Ulcers, goiter and high blood pressure are known as "stress diseases," the unfortunate, but growing, products of the stresses and strains of modern civilization. When life was calmer and more leisured, such diseases were very rare. With the rush and hurry of today, they are becoming more prevalent.

Unfortunately, they attack the most useful members of society. They are common among the more intelligent, ambitious and hard working. Those who are lazy, placid and without ambitions seldom suffer.

Hypnotism is helping, on an ever-growing scale, large numbers of sufferers from this group of diseases.

The hypnotist need possess no "mysterious gift" or "hypnotic power" whatever. Such a power, if it can be called that, lies within the subject or patient—the hypnotist merely has the technical knowledge of how to manipulate it.

PSYCHIATRIC USE OF HYPNOTISM EXPLAINED AT UNIVERSITY MEET

CHARLOTTESVILLE.—A John Hopkins Hospital physician told a psychiatry research conference here today how hypnotism has been used to help chronically ill patients.

Dr. Harold Rosen, of the Phipps Psychiatric Clinic at the Baltimore hospital, said patients were hypnotized without their knowledge so their symptoms could be better studied. During this state, he said, their symptoms were brought on or intensified so that real or apparent attacks of asthma or epilepsy were reproduced during a consultation.

By other methods, the formation of symptoms was blocked, Dr. Rosen said. With "the inevitable resultant anxiety reactions repressed," he said, . . . "underlying fantasies could erupt into conscious awareness even to the point of being acted out."

He gave an example: "An apparent, asthmatic patient, when his attack was blocked, acted out the killing of his girl friend." In another case, an epileptic patient acted in some ways like an infant."

The psychiatrist said, "By means of these techniques we have found it possible to determine the neurotic and psychotic functions which their symptoms serve. And whether or not it be asthma or epilepsy, either real or apparent, patients can be helped by psychotherapy."

Dr. Rosen admitted that "there is little in the whole field of treatment by hypnosis that is not controversial."

Rosen's talk was one of nine reports to the closing session of a meeting of psychiatrists and mental health workers from Virginia, Maryland, the Carolinas and the District of Columbia. The conference was jointly sponsored by the University of Virginia and the American Psychiatric Association.

In another report, Dr. Frank Lebar, of the University of North Carolina, told of his work at the Veterans Hospital at Roanoke in trying to help psychiatric patients make successful social adjustments when they return to their homes.

He explained how a ward is being set up in the 2,000-bed hospital to duplicate conditions which the patients will face when they leave the institution.

HYPNOSIS WIDENED IN THERAPEUTIC USE

Experts in Field Stress Value in Diagnosis of Cases for Psychiatric Treatment

NEW YORK.—Hypnotism promises to serve as an important adjunct in the therapy for certain ills largely emotional in origin, according to reports presented yesterday at the second annual scientific meeting of the Society for Clinical and Experimental Hypnosis.

The program at the New York Academy of Sciences included papers by specialists from the John Hopkins University School of

HYPNOTISM DOES HELP

Medicine, the University of Pennsylvania School of Medicine, the State University of New York College of Medicine and other leading institutions on the effects of hypnosis on body processes, the use of hypnotherapy in cases of depression and apparent focal epilepsy and in a child guidance clinic.

Dr. Jerome M. Schneck of the department of psychiatry, State University of New York College of Medicine, president of the society, who presided, observed that while most of the work with hypnotherapy in medical areas had been achieved in the field of psychiatry, "interesting explorations have been advanced in obstetrics and gynecology, dermatology, anethesiology, dentistry, internal medicine and in some aspects of surgery."

In Psychiatry For Children

A report prepared by Dr. Gordon Ambrose of London, which was read at the meeting, dealt with the use of hypnosis in the psychiatric treatment of children. Afflictions included nervousness, bed wetting, headaches, tics, vomiting and poor appetite. Such treatment, Dr. Schneck wrote, was often combined with counseling of the parents "in keeping with the more advanced type of psychiatric practice in child guidance clinics."

It was emphasized that hypnotism in itself did not serve as therapy, its potiential usefulness being in conjunction with standard medical procedures, psychotherapeutic or otherwise, just as anesthesia served to enable the qualified surgeon to operate.

One of its promising uses, it was noted, is as a diagnostic tool to help distinguish between ills of physical origin, requiring surgical or medical treatment, and those of purely emotional background that require psychiatric treatment.

Scientific hypnosis, said Dr. Schneck, "has weathered alternating periods of marked interest and relative neglect for very many years."

"Wartime experiences," he added, "have intensified concern with its medical aspects particularly because of the focusing of attention on the great numbers of psychiatric casualties."

The founding of the "Society for Clinical and Experimental Hypnosis," he said, "has served to centralize interchange of experiences concerning scientific hypnosis and to promote further investigations in this area of research."

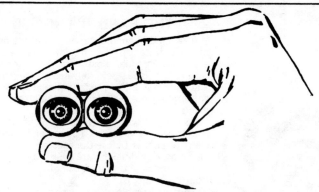

THE POWERS HYPNOTIC EYES

Here is an original technique that can be used very successfully in inducing hypnosis. The technique consists of using two glass eyes with eyelashes that close as you rotate the mechanism that holds the eyes in place. This action is similar to closing your eyes when falling asleep. You suggest to the subject as you hold these two eyes between your thumb and first finger that his eyes will become extremely heavy and tired as the eyes that you are holding begin to close. You then gradually begin to rotate your hand which causes the eyes to partially close. The subject, finding it extremely difficult to look at the eyes, begins to close his own eyes in unison with those that you are holding. You continue giving suggestions of hypnosis and before you know it the subject is under hypnosis. The eyes are the size of human eyes and are colored blue with brown eyelashes in order to give the exact effect of looking into real eyes.

The advantage comes in the fact that the subject begins to blink his eyes immediately and you suggest to him that this is the beginning of the hypnosis. It is just about impossible to look into anyone's eyes without blinking and this technique accomplishes this purpose. Using this knowledge, you incorporate it into your technique and induce the deep hypnosis accordingly. You can, of course, use this technique for self-hypnosis as well.

The Powers Hypnotic Eyes (1 pair)...$1

HYPNOTIC CRYSTAL BALL & CHAIN

I have had many request for a hypnotic crystal ball and chain. I finally have been able to secure these and am offering them now for the first time. The crystal ball measures one inch in diameter and is actually made of genuine methacrylate which is crystal clear. A ten-inch chain is secured to the crystal ball. You use this device the same as the regular crystal ball but this time you incorporate the pendulum effect which naturally causes the quick tiring of the eyes.

Professional Size—Hypnotic Crystal Ball & Chain ... $2.00

THE HAND HYPNODISC

The hand hypnodisc is the size of the hypnodisc illustrated in this circular. It is rigid with a special lens-like plastic surface. The miniature hypnodisc is held between the first finger and thumb like the crystal ball and is used incorporating the techniques of the large hypnodisc as well as the crystal ball.

As you slowly revolve this hypnodisc, the lens-like surface causes a series of optical illusions to appear before the eyes of the subject. These moving illusions are ever present as you change the slightest distance of the hypnodisc from the subject.

This remarkable effect is achieved by the use of countless plastic linear lenses which separate the multiple images laminated behind them, permitting a different picture to change continuously as you change the angle of view or distance. Naturally this device is extremely helpful in capturing the full attention of the conscious mind of the subject and helps you to achieve the hypnotic state in the shortest possible time.

Send for
THE HAND HYPNODISC
Price . . . $1

POWERS HYPNOTIC CRYSTAL BALL

The Powers hypnotic crystal ball is extremely useful as an aid in inducing the hypnotic state. It is desirable to use it as an object of concentration for your subject while he is being hypnotized.

The crystal ball lends an air of "mysticism" to the attainment of the hypnotic sleep and for some of your subjects this is the best approach in obtaining hypnotic control. There are individuals who will not react to a strict scientific approach to hypnosis and it is with these subjects that the use of such a device as the crystal ball is of inestimable value.

The crystal ball is held between your thumb and first finger, about twelve inches from the subject's eyes and slightly above eye level. The hypnotic crystal ball can easily be carried with you at all times.

As you know, the employment of a crystal to induce the hypnotic sleep is one of the oldest methods used in hypnosis. I personally favor this device and my students as well as myself have always had excellent results using this technique.

Send for POWERS HYPNOTIC CRYSTAL BALL

Price . . . $1

THE POWERS HYPNODISC

Copyright 1951 by Melvin Powers

An effective yet inexpensive method of inducing hypnosis is with the aid of the hypnodisc spiral. In my book, "Hypnotism Revealed," a picture of the hypnodisc unit with the hypnodisc spiral attached is shown. Above is a picture of my latest hypnodisc spiral. I am now offering the hypnodisc spiral as a separate unit which can be used with your phonograph turntable.

The spinning spiral will cause a series of optical illusions, causing immediate eye strain and fatigue. The subject feels that he is being drawn into a deep, dark revolving cone. By your suggestions of hypnotic sleep, you can place your subject in the somnambulistic state very easily. With some subjects, hypnosis will take place almost instantaneously. This technique is often employed in stage hypnotism.

The use of the hypnodisc spiral is also an excellent method of achieving self-hypnosis. As you concentrate on the revolving hypnodisc spiral, you give yourself suggestions of hypnotic sleep. You will note the optical illusions as they occur and the pleasant, relaxing feeling that accompanies these illusions. Giving yourself further suggestions of hypnotic sleep, you find that you are easily able to attain the desired state of self-hypnosis. This method is one of the most successful and popular techniques yet known for achieving heterohypnosis and self-hypnosis. At the Wilshire School of Hypnotism, all students in the self-hypnosis class are conditioned with the aid of the hypnodisc spiral.

During my lectures, I place the entire hypnodisc unit on the platform without having the spiral revolve. Continuing with the lecture, I note individuals in the audience gazing intently at the hypnodisc spiral. Invariably before the end of the lecture, many will have put themselves into a deep hypnotic state. This group self-hypnosis was achieved without my mentioning anything about the hypnodisc. These individuals assumed that the unit is used to induce hypnosis and their looking at it with that thought in mind produced the hypnotic state.

The hypnodisc spiral is printed on firm cardboard, measures twelve inches in diameter, and has a hole in the center so you can place it on your own phonograph turntable. It has the general appearance of a twelve-inch phonograph record. I am sure that you will be pleased with your purchase of the hypnodisc.

The hypnodisc is also available with four of the white spiraling areas colored in four different shades. The coloring is extremely interesting, fascinating, and very effective in inducing hypnosis as the hypnodisc revolves. The COLORED HYPNODISC sells for $3.00.

Send for POWERS HYPNODISC
Price . . . $2.00

CASSETTE TAPES

ONE HOUR HYPNOTIC RECORDS ON CASSETTE TAPE $10.00

ONE HOUR HYPNOTIC RAIN RECORD ON CASSETTE TAPE 5.00

TWO HOURS OF MENTAL POWER RECORDS ON CASSETTE TAPE 10.00

ONE HOUR HYPNOTIC RAIN TAPE (3¾ IPS)

One of the chief assets of a good hypnotist is to be flexible in his approach in hypnotizing his subjects. As you know, it is necessary many times to adapt a technique that is suitable to the subject, and not to make the subject adapt himself to the method of induction.

We know that with somnambulistic subjects any procedure will put the subject under hypnosis immediately. The hypnotist gains complete control of his subject just as fast as he wants. Unfortunately, most subjects do not respond at the first session because of conscious or subconscious fears that must be gradually eliminated. Once you get the subject to relax, or "let go," he will naturally succumb to hypnosis. This is the problem that confronts all hypnotists.

Merely suggesting to the subject to relax or to "let go" is not sufficient, as a rule, to bring about this desired state. The subject, at this point, cannot turn on or off his mental and physical state of being this easily. Even if we have the subject lie down, this does not assure the hypnotic state, as the subject can still be tense. Our problem is how to get the subject to relax. Our situation is similar to the physician telling his patient to go home and forget about a certain problem. I'm sure that you'll agree that the advice is virtually impossible to follow.

One of the major stumbling blocks in hypnotizing a subject, or in self-hypnosis, lies in the fact that although we use words such as: "relax," "let yourself go," and other similar terminology, the subject cannot readily put the meaning of these words into effect. It is difficult for most people to "let go" when we live in a society that beckons us to "look sharp," "be sharp," "be alert," "be on the ball" and "make every minute count." Emphasis on productivity does not lend to a society of relaxed individuals.

In my long experience as a professional hypnotist, I have tried many novel innovations for inducing hypnosis. Some have met with a great deal of success and others have failed. It is difficult to determine the causative factors for success or failure. We can only theorize.

I have used, over the last ten years, a technique that I shall describe now. Exceptionally good results have been attained with it; however, it is not infallible. It is suggested to you as another good technique. In order to help the subject relax, I have been using a one hour tape recorder recording containing the continuous sound of various degrees of rain. One half hour has a rain effect of very soft, light rainfall, as on grass, canvas or tent top. The other side contains a half hour of a rain effect such as one would hear in a heavy downfall with prominent patter of water on pavement.

The subject is instructed to close his eyes and listen to the sound of the rain while picturing himself relaxing near a warm, glowing fireplace. The relaxing effect thus produced enhances our chances for success in attaining a deep, hypnotic state.

The tape will play on all standard recorders and comes recorded at a speed of 3¾ IPS. The tape alone is worth $2.50. You therefore only pay $2.50 for the actual recording. **ONE HOUR HYPNOTIC RAIN TAPE ... $**

A PERSONAL WORD FROM MELVIN POWERS
PUBLISHER, WILSHIRE BOOK COMPANY

Dear Friend:

My goal is to publish interesting, informative, and inspirational books. You can help me accomplish this by answering the following questions, either by phone or by mail. Or, if convenient for you, I would welcome the opportunity to visit with you in my office and hear your comments in person.

Did you enjoy reading this book? Why?

Would you enjoy reading another similar book?

What idea in the book impressed you the most?

If applicable to your situation, have you incorporated this idea in your daily life?

Is there a chapter that could serve as a theme for an entire book? Please explain.

If you have an idea for a book, I would welcome discussing it with you. If you already have one in progress, write or call me concerning possible publication. I can be reached at (213) 875-1711 or (213) 983-1105.

Sincerely yours,

MELVIN POWERS

12015 Sherman Road
North Hollywood, California 91605

MELVIN POWERS SELF-IMPROVEMENT LIBRARY

ASTROLOGY

____ASTROLOGY: HOW TO CHART YOUR HOROSCOPE *Max Heindel*		3.00
____ASTROLOGY: YOUR PERSONAL SUN-SIGN GUIDE *Beatrice Ryder*		3.00
____ASTROLOGY FOR EVERYDAY LIVING *Janet Harris*		2.00
____ASTROLOGY MADE EASY *Astarte*		3.00
____ASTROLOGY MADE PRACTICAL *Alexandra Kayhle*		3.00
____ASTROLOGY, ROMANCE, YOU AND THE STARS *Anthony Norvell*		4.00
____MY WORLD OF ASTROLOGY *Sydney Omarr*		5.00
____THOUGHT DIAL *Sydney Omarr*		3.00
____WHAT THE STARS REVEAL ABOUT THE MEN IN YOUR LIFE *Thelma White*		3.00

BRIDGE

____BRIDGE BIDDING MADE EASY *Edwin B. Kantar*	5.00
____BRIDGE CONVENTIONS *Edwin B. Kantar*	5.00
____BRIDGE HUMOR *Edwin B. Kantar*	3.00
____COMPETITIVE BIDDING IN MODERN BRIDGE *Edgar Kaplan*	4.00
____DEFENSIVE BRIDGE PLAY COMPLETE *Edwin B. Kantar*	10.00
____HOW TO IMPROVE YOUR BRIDGE *Alfred Sheinwold*	3.00
____IMPROVING YOUR BIDDING SKILLS *Edwin B. Kantar*	4.00
____INTRODUCTION TO DEFENDER'S PLAY *Edwin B. Kantar*	3.00
____SHORT CUT TO WINNING BRIDGE *Alfred Sheinwold*	3.00
____TEST YOUR BRIDGE PLAY *Edwin B. Kantar*	3.00
____WINNING DECLARER PLAY *Dorothy Hayden Truscott*	4.00

BUSINESS, STUDY & REFERENCE

____CONVERSATION MADE EASY *Elliot Russell*	2.00
____EXAM SECRET *Dennis B. Jackson*	2.00
____FIX-IT BOOK *Arthur Symons*	2.00
____HOW TO DEVELOP A BETTER SPEAKING VOICE *M. Hellier*	2.00
____HOW TO MAKE A FORTUNE IN REAL ESTATE *Albert Winnikoff*	4.00
____INCREASE YOUR LEARNING POWER *Geoffrey A. Dudley*	2.00
____MAGIC QF NUMBERS *Robert Tocquet*	2.00
____PRACTICAL GUIDE TO BETTER CONCENTRATION *Melvin Powers*	2.00
____PRACTICAL GUIDE TO PUBLIC SPEAKING *Maurice Forley*	3.00
____7 DAYS TO FASTER READING *William S. Schaill*	3.00
____SONGWRITERS RHYMING DICTIONARY *Jane Shaw Whitfield*	5.00
____SPELLING MADE EASY *Lester D. Basch & Dr. Milton Finkelstein*	2.00
____STUDENT'S GUIDE TO BETTER GRADES *J. A. Rickard*	3.00
____TEST YOURSELF—Find Your Hidden Talent *Jack Shafer*	2.00
____YOUR WILL & WHAT TO DO ABOUT IT *Attorney Samuel G. Kling*	3.00

CALLIGRAPHY

____ADVANCED CALLIGRAPHY *Katherine Jeffares*	6.00
____CALLIGRAPHY—The Art of Beautiful Writing *Katherine Jeffares*	5.00

CHESS & CHECKERS

____BEGINNER'S GUIDE TO WINNING CHESS *Fred Reinfeld*	3.00
____BETTER CHESS—How to Play *Fred Reinfeld*	2.00
____CHECKERS MADE EASY *Tom Wiswell*	2.00
____CHESS IN TEN EASY LESSONS *Larry Evans*	3.00
____CHESS MADE EASY *Milton L. Hanauer*	3.00
____CHESS MASTERY—A New Approach *Fred Reinfeld*	2.00
____CHESS PROBLEMS FOR BEGINNERS *edited by Fred Reinfeld*	2.00
____CHESS SECRETS REVEALED *Fred Reinfeld*	2.00
____CHESS STRATEGY—An Expert's Guide *Fred Reinfeld*	2.00
____CHESS TACTICS FOR BEGINNERS *edited by Fred Reinfeld*	3.00
____CHESS THEORY & PRACTICE *Morry & Mitchell*	2.00
____HOW TO WIN AT CHECKERS *Fred Reinfeld*	2.00
____1001 BRILLIANT WAYS TO CHECKMATE *Fred Reinfeld*	3.00
____1001 WINNING CHESS SACRIFICES & COMBINATIONS *Fred Reinfeld*	3.00
____SOVIET CHESS *Edited by R. G. Wade*	3.00

COOKERY & HERBS

____CULPEPER'S HERBAL REMEDIES *Dr. Nicholas Culpeper*	2.00

PAYDAY AT THE RACES *Les Conklin*	3.00
SMART HANDICAPPING MADE EASY *William Bauman*	3.00
SUCCESS AT THE HARNESS RACES *Barry Meadow*	3.00
WINNING AT THE HARNESS RACES—An Expert's Guide *Nick Cammarano*	3.00

HUMOR

HOW TO BE A COMEDIAN FOR FUN & PROFIT *King & Laufer*	2.00
HOW TO FLATTEN YOUR TUSH *Coach Marge Reardon*	2.00
JOKE TELLER'S HANDBOOK *Bob Orben*	3.00
JOKES FOR ALL OCCASIONS *Al Schock*	3.00
2000 NEW LAUGHS FOR SPEAKERS *Bob Orben*	3.00

HYPNOTISM

ADVANCED TECHNIQUES OF HYPNOSIS *Melvin Powers*	2.00
BRAINWASHING AND THE CULTS *Paul A. Verdier, Ph.D.*	3.00
CHILDBIRTH WITH HYPNOSIS *William S. Kroger, M.D.*	3.00
HOW TO SOLVE Your Sex Problems with Self-Hypnosis *Frank S. Caprio, M.D.*	3.00
HOW TO STOP SMOKING THRU SELF-HYPNOSIS *Leslie M. LeCron*	3.00
HOW TO USE AUTO-SUGGESTION EFFECTIVELY *John Duckworth*	3.00
HOW YOU CAN BOWL BETTER USING SELF-HYPNOSIS *Jack Heise*	3.00
HOW YOU CAN PLAY BETTER GOLF USING SELF-HYPNOSIS *Jack Heise*	2.00
HYPNOSIS AND SELF-HYPNOSIS *Bernard Hollander, M.D.*	3.00
HYPNOTISM *(Originally published in 1893) Carl Sextus*	3.00
HYPNOTISM & PSYCHIC PHENOMENA *Simeon Edmunds*	3.00
HYPNOTISM MADE EASY *Dr. Ralph Winn*	3.00
HYPNOTISM MADE PRACTICAL *Louis Orton*	3.00
HYPNOTISM REVEALED *Melvin Powers*	2.00
HYPNOTISM TODAY *Leslie LeCron and Jean Bordeaux, Ph.D.*	4.00
MODERN HYPNOSIS *Lesley Kuhn & Salvatore Russo, Ph.D.*	5.00
NEW CONCEPTS OF HYPNOSIS *Bernard C. Gindes, M.D.*	4.00
NEW SELF-HYPNOSIS *Paul Adams*	3.00
POST-HYPNOTIC INSTRUCTIONS—Suggestions for Therapy *Arnold Furst*	3.00
PRACTICAL GUIDE TO SELF-HYPNOSIS *Melvin Powers*	3.00
PRACTICAL HYPNOTISM *Philip Magonet, M.D.*	2.00
SECRETS OF HYPNOTISM *S. J. Van Pelt, M.D.*	3.00
SELF-HYPNOSIS A Conditioned-Response Technique *Laurance Sparks*	4.00
SELF-HYPNOSIS Its Theory, Technique & Application *Melvin Powers*	3.00
THERAPY THROUGH HYPNOSIS *edited by Raphael H. Rhodes*	4.00

JUDAICA

HOW TO LIVE A RICHER & FULLER LIFE *Rabbi Edgar F. Magnin*	2.00
MODERN ISRAEL *Lily Edelman*	2.00
ROMANCE OF HASSIDISM *Jacob S. Minkin*	2.50
SERVICE OF THE HEART *Evelyn Garfiel, Ph.D.*	4.00
STORY OF ISRAEL IN COINS *Jean & Maurice Gould*	2.00
STORY OF ISRAEL IN STAMPS *Maxim & Gabriel Shamir*	1.00
TREASURY OF COMFORT *edited by Rabbi Sidney Greenberg*	4.00

JUST FOR WOMEN

COSMOPOLITAN'S GUIDE TO MARVELOUS MEN Fwd. by *Helen Gurley Brown*	3.00
COSMOPOLITAN'S HANG-UP HANDBOOK Foreword by *Helen Gurley Brown*	4.00
COSMOPOLITAN'S LOVE BOOK—A Guide to Ecstasy in Bed	3.00
COSMOPOLITAN'S NEW ETIQUETTE GUIDE Fwd. by *Helen Gurley Brown*	4.00
I AM A COMPLEAT WOMAN *Doris Hagopian & Karen O'Connor Sweeney*	3.00
JUST FOR WOMEN—A Guide to the Female Body *Richard E. Sand, M.D.*	4.00
NEW APPROACHES TO SEX IN MARRIAGE *John E. Eichenlaub, M.D.*	3.00
SEXUALLY ADEQUATE FEMALE *Frank S. Caprio, M.D.*	3.00
YOUR FIRST YEAR OF MARRIAGE *Dr. Tom McGinnis*	3.00

MARRIAGE, SEX & PARENTHOOD

ABILITY TO LOVE *Dr. Allan Fromme*	5.00
ENCYCLOPEDIA OF MODERN SEX & LOVE TECHNIQUES *Macandrew*	4.00
GUIDE TO SUCCESSFUL MARRIAGE *Drs. Albert Ellis & Robert Harper*	4.00
HOW TO RAISE AN EMOTIONALLY HEALTHY, HAPPY CHILD *A. Ellis*	3.00
IMPOTENCE & FRIGIDITY *Edwin W. Hirsch, M.D.*	3.00
SEX WITHOUT GUILT *Albert Ellis, Ph.D.*	3.00
SEXUALLY ADEQUATE MALE *Frank S. Caprio, M.D.*	3.00

____MAGIC IN YOUR MIND *U. S. Andersen*	4.00
____MAGIC OF THINKING BIG *Dr. David J. Schwartz*	3.00
____MAGIC POWER OF YOUR MIND *Walter M. Germain*	4.00
____MENTAL POWER THROUGH SLEEP SUGGESTION *Melvin Powers*	2.00
____NEW GUIDE TO RATIONAL LIVING *Albert Ellis, Ph.D. & R. Harper, Ph.D.*	3.00
____OUR TROUBLED SELVES *Dr. Allan Fromme*	3.00
____PSYCHO-CYBERNETICS *Maxwell Maltz, M.D.*	2.00
____SCIENCE OF MIND IN DAILY LIVING *Dr. Donald Curtis*	3.00
____SECRET OF SECRETS *U. S. Andersen*	4.00
____SECRET POWER OF THE PYRAMIDS *U. S. Andersen*	4.00
____STUTTERING AND WHAT YOU CAN DO ABOUT IT *W. Johnson, Ph.D.*	2.50
____SUCCESS-CYBERNETICS *U. S. Andersen*	4.00
____10 DAYS TO A GREAT NEW LIFE *William E. Edwards*	3.00
____THINK AND GROW RICH *Napoleon Hill*	3.00
____THREE MAGIC WORDS *U. S. Andersen*	4.00
____TREASURY OF THE ART OF LIVING *Sidney S. Greenberg*	5.00
____YOU ARE NOT THE TARGET *Laura Huxley*	3.00
____YOUR SUBCONSCIOUS POWER *Charles M. Simmons*	4.00
____YOUR THOUGHTS CAN CHANGE YOUR LIFE *Dr. Donald Curtis*	3.00

SPORTS

____ARCHERY—An Expert's Guide *Dan Stamp*	2.00
____BICYCLING FOR FUN AND GOOD HEALTH *Kenneth E. Luther*	2.00
____BILLIARDS—Pocket • Carom • Three Cushion *Clive Cottingham, Jr.*	3.00
____CAMPING-OUT 101 Ideas & Activities *Bruno Knobel*	2.00
____COMPLETE GUIDE TO FISHING *Vlad Evanoff*	2.00
____HOW TO IMPROVE YOUR RACQUETBALL *Lubarsky, Kaufman, & Scagnetti*	3.00
____HOW TO WIN AT POCKET BILLIARDS *Edward D. Knuchell*	3.00
____JOY OF WALKING *Jack Scagnetti*	3.00
____LEARNING & TEACHING SOCCER SKILLS *Eric Worthington*	3.00
____MOTORCYCLING FOR BEGINNERS *I. G. Edmonds*	3.00
____RACQUETBALL MADE EASY *Steve Lubarsky, Rod Delson & Jack Scagnetti*	3.00
____SECRET OF BOWLING STRIKES *Dawson Taylor*	3.00
____SECRET OF PERFECT PUTTING *Horton Smith & Dawson Taylor*	3.00
____SOCCER—The game & how to play it *Gary Rosenthal*	3.00
____STARTING SOCCER *Edward F. Dolan, Jr.*	3.00
____TABLE TENNIS MADE EASY *Johnny Leach*	2.00

TENNIS LOVERS' LIBRARY

____BEGINNER'S GUIDE TO WINNING TENNIS *Helen Hull Jacobs*	2.00
____HOW TO BEAT BETTER TENNIS PLAYERS *Loring Fiske*	4.00
____HOW TO IMPROVE YOUR TENNIS—Style, Strategy & Analysis *C. Wilson*	2.00
____INSIDE TENNIS—Techniques of Winning *Jim Leighton*	3.00
____PLAY TENNIS WITH ROSEWALL *Ken Rosewall*	2.00
____PSYCH YOURSELF TO BETTER TENNIS *Dr. Walter A. Luszki*	2.00
____SUCCESSFUL TENNIS *Neale Fraser*	2.00
____TENNIS FOR BEGINNERS *Dr. H. A. Murray*	2.00
____TENNIS MADE EASY *Joel Brecheen*	2.00
____WEEKEND TENNIS—How to have fun & win at the same time *Bill Talbert*	3.00
____WINNING WITH PERCENTAGE TENNIS—Smart Strategy *Jack Lowe*	2.00

WILSHIRE PET LIBRARY

____DOG OBEDIENCE TRAINING *Gust Kessopulos*	3.00
____DOG TRAINING MADE EASY & FUN *John W. Kellogg*	3.00
____HOW TO BRING UP YOUR PET DOG *Kurt Unkelbach*	2.00
____HOW TO RAISE & TRAIN YOUR PUPPY *Jeff Griffen*	2.00
____PIGEONS: HOW TO RAISE & TRAIN THEM *William H. Allen, Jr.*	2.00

WILSHIRE HORSE LOVERS' LIBRARY

____AMATEUR HORSE BREEDER *A. C. Leighton Hardman*	3.00
____AMERICAN QUARTER HORSE IN PICTURES *Margaret Cabell Self*	3.00
____APPALOOSA HORSE *Donna & Bill Richardson*	3.00
____ARABIAN HORSE *Reginald S. Summerhays*	2.00
____ART OF WESTERN RIDING *Suzanne Norton Jones*	3.00
____AT THE HORSE SHOW *Margaret Cabell Self*	3.00
____BACK-YARD FOAL *Peggy Jett Pittinger*	3.00
____BACK-YARD HORSE *Peggy Jett Pittinger*	3.00
____BASIC DRESSAGE *Jean Froissard*	2.00
____BEGINNER'S GUIDE TO HORSEBACK RIDING *Sheila Wall*	2.00
____BEGINNER'S GUIDE TO THE WESTERN HORSE *Natlee Kenoyer*	2.00
____BITS—THEIR HISTORY, USE AND MISUSE *Louis Taylor*	3.00
____BREAKING & TRAINING THE DRIVING HORSE *Doris Ganton*	2.00
____BREAKING YOUR HORSE'S BAD HABITS *W. Dayton Sumner*	3.00
____CAVALRY MANUAL OF HORSEMANSHIP *Gordon Wright*	3.00
____COMPLETE TRAINING OF HORSE AND RIDER *Colonel Alois Podhajsky*	4.00
____DISORDERS OF THE HORSE & WHAT TO DO ABOUT THEM *E. Hanauer*	3.00
____DOG TRAINING MADE EASY & FUN *John W. Kellogg*	3.00
____DRESSAGE—A Study of the Finer Points in Riding *Henry Wynmalen*	4.00
____DRIVING HORSES *Sallie Walrond*	3.00
____ENDURANCE RIDING *Ann Hyland*	2.00
____EQUITATION *Jean Froissard*	4.00
____FIRST AID FOR HORSES *Dr. Charles H. Denning, Jr.*	2.00
____FUN OF RAISING A COLT *Rubye & Frank Griffith*	3.00
____FUN ON HORSEBACK *Margaret Cabell Self*	4.00
____GYMKHANA GAMES *Natlee Kenoyer*	2.00
____HORSE DISEASES—Causes, Symptoms & Treatment *Dr. H. G. Belschner*	3.00
____HORSE OWNER'S CONCISE GUIDE *Elsie V. Hanauer*	2.00
____HORSE SELECTION & CARE FOR BEGINNERS *George H. Conn*	3.00
____HORSE SENSE—A complete guide to riding and care *Alan Deacon*	4.00
____HORSEBACK RIDING FOR BEGINNERS *Louis Taylor*	4.00
____HORSEBACK RIDING MADE EASY & FUN *Sue Henderson Coen*	3.00
____HORSES—Their Selection, Care & Handling *Margaret Cabell Self*	3.00
____HOW TO BUY A BETTER HORSE & SELL THE HORSE YOU OWN	3.00
____HOW TO ENJOY YOUR QUARTER HORSE *Williard H. Porter*	3.00
____HUNTER IN PICTURES *Margaret Cabell Self*	2.00
____ILLUSTRATED BOOK OF THE HORSE *S. Sidney* (8½" x 11")	10.00
____ILLUSTRATED HORSE MANAGEMENT—400 Illustrations *Dr. E. Mayhew*	6.00
____ILLUSTRATED HORSE TRAINING *Captain M. H. Hayes*	5.00
____ILLUSTRATED HORSEBACK RIDING FOR BEGINNERS *Jeanne Mellin*	2.00
____JUMPING—Learning & Teaching *Jean Froissard*	3.00
____KNOW ALL ABOUT HORSES *Harry Disston*	3.00
____LAME HORSE—Causes, Symptoms & Treatment *Dr. James R. Rooney*	3.00
____LAW & YOUR HORSE *Edward H. Greene*	3.00
____LIPIZZANERS & THE SPANISH RIDING SCHOOL *W. Reuter* (4¼" x 6")	2.50
____MANUAL OF HORSEMANSHIP *Harold Black*	5.00
____MORGAN HORSE IN PICTURES *Margaret Cabell Self*	2.00
____MOVIE HORSES—The Fascinating Techniques of Training *Anthony Amaral*	2.00
____POLICE HORSES *Judith Campbell*	2.00
____PRACTICAL GUIDE TO HORSESHOEING	3.00
____PRACTICAL GUIDE TO OWNING YOUR OWN HORSE *Steven D. Price*	2.00
____PRACTICAL HORSE PSYCHOLOGY *Moyra Williams*	3.00
____PROBLEM HORSES Guide for Curing Serious Behavior Habits *Summerhays*	2.00
____REINSMAN OF THE WEST—BRIDLES & BITS *Ed Connell*	4.00
____RESCHOOLING THE THOROUGHBRED *Peggy Jett Pittenger*	3.00
____RIDE WESTERN *Louis Taylor*	3.00
____SCHOOLING YOUR YOUNG HORSE *George Wheatley*	2.00
____STABLE MANAGEMENT FOR THE OWNER-GROOM *George Wheatley*	4.00
____STALLION MANAGEMENT—A Guide for Stud Owners *A. C. Hardman*	3.00
____TEACHING YOUR HORSE TO JUMP *W. J. Froud*	2.00
____TRAIL HORSES & TRAIL RIDING *Anne & Perry Westbrook*	2.00
____TRAINING YOUR HORSE TO SHOW *Neale Haley*	3.00
____TREATING COMMON DISEASES OF YOUR HORSE *Dr. George H. Conn*	3.00
____TREATING HORSE AILMENTS *G. W. Serth*	2.00
____WESTERN HORSEBACK RIDING *Glen Balch*	3.00
____YOU AND YOUR PONY *Pepper Mainwaring Healey* (8½" x 11")	6.00
____YOUR FIRST HORSE *George C. Saunders, M.D.*	3.00
____YOUR PONY BOOK *Hermann Wiederhold*	2.00
____YOUR WESTERN HORSE *Nelson C. Nye*	2.00

*The books listed above can be obtained from your book dealer or directly from
Melvin Powers. When ordering, please remit 50¢ per book postage & handling.
Send for our free illustrated catalog of self-improvement books.*

Melvin Powers
12015 Sherman Road, No. Hollywood, California 91605

NOTES

NOTES

NOTES

NOTES